Life Hacks for ChatGPT Beginners

Life Hacks for ChatGPT Beginners

501 Prompts to Make Your Life Easier

Stanley Lieber

Callisto Publishing LLC

Published by Callisto Publishing LLC C/O Sourcebooks LLC
1935 Brookdale Rd, Suite 139, Naperville, IL 60563
(630) 961-3900
callistopublishing.com

Copyright © 2026 by Callisto Publishing LLC
Text by Stanley Lieber
Illustrations © nadia_bormotova/iStock/Getty Images with the following exception:
© phototechno/DigitalVision Vectors/Getty Images: throughout (dash pattern)
Cover and internal design © 2026 by Callisto Publishing LLC

All rights reserved. At Callisto, we believe that books change lives. Thank you for buying an authorized copy of this book. Please note that no part of this book may be used or reproduced in any manner for the purpose of training artificial intelligence technologies or systems.

Callisto and the colophon are trademarks of Callisto Publishing LLC.

Art Director: Lisa Schreiber
Art Producer: Stacey Stambaugh
Editor: Mo Mozuch
Production Editor: Rachel Taenzler
Production Designer: Jeffrey Piekarz

This publication is designed to provide accurate and authoritative information in regard to the subject matter covered. It is sold with the understanding that the publisher is not engaged in rendering legal, accounting, or other professional service. If legal advice or other expert assistance is required, the services of a competent professional person should be sought. —*From a Declaration of Principles Jointly Adopted by a Committee of the American Bar Association and a Committee of Publishers and Associations*

All brand names and product names used in this book are trademarks, registered trademarks, or trade names of their respective holders. Callisto Publishing is not associated with any product or vendor in this book.

Cataloging-in-Publication Data is on file with the Library of Congress.

Printed and bound in the United States of America
VP 10 9 8 7 6 5 4 3 2 1

Contents

Introduction

Technology moves fast. One minute, there's a rotary telephone in your kitchen, and the next your kid is texting you about chatbots doing their homework. Keeping up with the new ways machines influence our lives can be a bit daunting, which is why I've been tasked to write this book for you. I've been writing articles about technology and the internet for the past decade, explaining everything from air purifiers to social media algorithms. And in this book, I'm going to demystify the latest trend, ChatGPT. You'll learn what it is, how it works and, most important, how to use it to improve your life.

Artificial Intelligence (AI) assistants like ChatGPT have evolved from simple technological gimmicks to some of the most useful tools online. These versions of AI are not hell-bent on enslaving humanity, unlike how artificial intelligence is portrayed in many movies.

ChatGPT can answer questions, streamline tasks, or just write goofy songs based on "prompts"—basic queries—from users. But staring at a blank prompt box with nearly infinite possibilities can be daunting to anyone who's never dabbled in this space. This book is here to help you feel comfortable experimenting with this new tool. The robot learning program can't judge you, and there's no prompt too simple or obtuse. Just open the program and start typing, and with our help, soon you'll be an expert prompter using ChatGPT to its fullest potential.

This book isn't designed by someone from Silicon Valley who has been maximizing his sleep and productivity schedules while subsisting solely on liquid food and libertarian dreams. I'm a tech enthusiast who enjoys the potential of new technology to improve the lives of the average person in any way possible. This book will help you get the most out of ChatGPT without being overwhelmed.

How to Use This Book

This book is packed with prompts and questions, across many different categories, that you can ask ChatGPT. Reading through part 1 will give you a comprehensive education on ChatGPT and how it can be used to improve your everyday life. Or, you can choose to skip all the history and tips and jump straight into the curated prompts and phrases in part 2 that you can feed directly into the program or use as templates you can modify to meet your needs.

PART ONE

Understanding ChatGPT

To use ChatGPT, you don't need to know exactly how it magically turns your words into new ideas and solutions. But like any tool you'd keep around the house, it's important to understand what it's designed for to get the most out of it. Your first impression may be that ChatGPT is a monolith that will turn any of your words into full-fledged projects. Though it appears the app can do anything, there are some limitations you'll need to learn too.

In part 1, we will explain how ChatGPT was born, what it can and cannot do, and the ethical quandaries that surround it. We won't go too deep into the weeds, but it's important to keep an open mind and not let the weight of this technological marvel get in the way of the fun you can have with it.

hey
ask me anything

Chapter 1

What Is ChatGPT?

This chapter will provide a crash course in defining ChatGPT. When used correctly, ChatGPT can offer a slew of benefits that can change your life. But it must be treated fairly and used properly to produce the most effective content and answers. If you get frustrated and think you can spend hours yelling at ChatGPT in all caps to try to get a better answer, you'll end up worse off than you were before you started. Using the program effectively isn't difficult, but you do need to know when to stay the course and when to change your approach.

WHY SHOULD YOU CARE ABOUT CHATGPT?

At its core, ChatGPT is a program that uses a massive collection of information, from both the internet and other users. AI programs all follow a similar path, using this collected data and learning from it. It's a lot like Google or other search engines, but instead of searching for specific keywords, it does its version of thinking to solve and share.

ChatGPT offers many users a way to streamline their lives, come up with creative solutions to dilemmas, or just have fun. It's a tool like any other. The more you learn and the more you practice, the better the results will be. A few decades ago, a program that could plan your calendar while reading your poetry would have been science fiction. But now that it's here, you should be excited about trying it and learning what it can and cannot do.

What ChatGPT Cannot Do

Though ChatGPT can do a lot, it does have limits. It also won't always be correct, which is why it's important to double-check the sources it is pulling information from. It can even "hallucinate," thinking it knows the answer to a question when it's actually sharing the wrong information.

Though its pool of information is massive, it can't pull from everything that's ever been created, so there are a few places it can't reach. Nothing it does is creative; instead, it remixes data from the web into new sentences.

Also, it may not have a logical understanding of a problem, but it could be overconfident even when it's wrong. A misstep early on in ChatGPT's lifespan went viral when it said the best way to keep cheese on a slippery pizza is glue, even when you know that Elmer's doesn't exactly make a good condiment.

Also, if you have an incredibly long conversation with ChatGPT, it might not be able to remember all of the information you've given it. Just like a person, if you drone on and on in a casual conversation, it will struggle to keep up.

What You Shouldn't Do with ChatGPT

Breaking the rules in OpenAI's terms of use for ChatGPT could lead to your account being deleted, and there are also other ethical and legal boundaries to be aware of:

- Don't share your personal or financial information. That information will be added to ChatGPT's catalog and can be used by bad actors to steal your private data.
- Don't use ChatGPT as your only source for a medical diagnosis. You should always consult a physician rather than an AI chatbot for any of your medical issues.
- Don't use it as your sole source of legal advice. ChatGPT did not pass the bar exam.

- Don't rely on it for financial guidance. It may seem appealing to have ChatGPT choose your stock portfolio, but its information could be wrong or outdated and throw you into financial ruin.
- Don't replace your therapist with ChatGPT. Though it might be nice to have a voice that can listen to your needs, you should contact a mental health professional if you are in crisis.
- Don't rely on ChatGPT for breaking news. The algorithm will not be up-to-date on events as they are happening.
- Don't use it to replace your expert judgment when making decisions. Do not rely solely on ChatGPT for anything that will seriously impact your life.
- Don't let ChatGPT teach your kids without supervision. You shouldn't let young children roam the internet completely alone; that's how they end up watching the really weird *Minecraft* videos.
- Don't use it to write essays or complete schoolwork. Having ChatGPT do all your writing for you may sound appealing, but new programs pop up every day that teachers can use to detect AI-written content (also, you shouldn't cheat).

What Are ChatGPT Life Hacks?

Say you have a garden in your backyard, and your tomato plants keep dying. Year after year, you try to grow delicious, juicy fruits to put on your salads, but all you end up with is mush, half-eaten sprouts, or a big pile of dirt. You can use ChatGPT to help plan when you should plant, come up with a strategy to deal with pests, or just pivot to a vegetable that will grow even with your brown thumb.

ChatGPT can offer solutions that you never would have thought of. Adding a prompt search to parts of your daily routine can make tasks that you found impossible just a bit easier. For example, I've started using ChatGPT to plan my meal prep for the week. I tell it what ingredients I have, how much protein and how many calories I want to eat, and how much time I have to prepare the meals. It comes up with a plan that, after some recipe testing, results in delicious and nutritious meals.

ChatGPT-assisted life hacks can range from the incredibly simple to intricate curations of your day-to-day activities. It's all about making your existence easier and automating routine tasks, giving you more time to do the things you enjoy. As our lives become more complex, we have less free time, so it's nice to have an AI buddy that can simplify tasks and responsibilities. These life hacks aren't meant to replace your input or knowledge but rather to supplement your skills to make life much easier.

A BRIEF HISTORY OF AI CHAT MODELS

Over the past sixty years, AI chat models have evolved from simple machines to the incredibly complex neural networks we see today. In 1966, Joseph Weizenbaum, while at MIT, invented ELIZA, a program known as a "chatbot" that was designed to approximate human conversation. ELIZA was meant to deceive its human users into thinking they were chatting with a real person. It mimicked a therapist, responding with open-ended questions and repeating back phrases that were fed into it.

Over the next few decades, chatbot technology would slowly start to improve. In 1972, American psychiatrist Kenneth Colby constructed PARRY, which imitated a patient with schizophrenia. In 1988, British computer scientist Rollo Carpenter aimed to create a natural human conversationalist with Jabberwacky. In 1991, Creative Labs introduced Dr. Sbaitso, which is considered the first chatbot to incorporate artificial intelligence and full voice operation.

But in the first decade of the 2000s, things really started to kick into overdrive. ALICE (an acronym for *artificial linguistic internet computer entity*) is the foundational technology found in most of today's chatbots, using pattern recognition to come off convincingly as a human in conversation. In 2010, the world was introduced to Apple's Siri, and it was most likely the first chatbot you ever interacted with when you asked Siri to turn the volume down on your speaker or set a reminder for the next day.

In 2016, the modern AI boom took off. Now the technology is being integrated into almost everything in our day-to-day lives. More companies started putting their chatbots inside smart devices, like Amazon's Alexa and Microsoft's Cortana. ChatGPT launched its chatbot in November 2022, creating a tidal wave of chatbots that are being developed, refined, and released.

PROS AND CONS OF CHATGPT

ChatGPT is highly versatile and can be tweaked to fit your needs or wants, but it can also deliver incorrect answers or misunderstand your prompts. As with all tools, it's important to understand ChatGPT's abilities and drawbacks so you can get the best results.

As an emerging technology, ChatGPT is constantly evolving and changing. As old issues get fixed, new ones arise. The information in this section reflects the functionality of current ChatGPT models at the time of publication.

Pro: Fast and Effective

It might take you minutes or even hours to come up with a solution to a problem, but ChatGPT can arrive at an answer in seconds. Its instant responses make research or content generation a breeze, allowing you to spend time working on other tasks. For example, a student can feed a complex academic paper into the algorithm and summarize its important points in record time. ChatGPT can organize and reorganize lists that would require a tedious amount of typing and formatting. That speed is ultimately what makes ChatGPT valuable to the user because it turns difficult, time-consuming tasks into simple button presses.

Pro: Ultimate Brainstorming Tool

As a writer, I sometimes find it difficult to come up with new topics and fresh angles. But ChatGPT makes brainstorming much easier, allowing me to input a prompt that instantly curates the information my story should convey. By synthesizing my prompts with its vast amount of human knowledge, ChatGPT can come up with ways to explore topics I never thought possible. This goes far beyond writing and can help you brainstorm for vacations, events, or work-related projects.

Pro: You Can Talk to It Like It's a Person

When you type into Google or another search engine, you have to be very specific with the keywords you use to get the best answer, but ChatGPT is more advanced than your average website. In fact, you'll find your ChatGPT sessions most successful if you just talk to it like a regular person. Once it begins to learn more about how you like to communicate, its responses and follow-ups will sound so organic that it can be hard to remember you are talking to a robot. But it *is* just a robot, as the following list of drawbacks will illustrate.

Con: AI Hallucinations

When you ask ChatGPT a question, it combs through every piece of information to which it has access to come up with what it calculates is the correct result. ChatGPT is programmed to prioritize giving you an answer, so much so that it can sometimes reach too far. Lawyers have been caught using ChatGPT to make briefs that cite court cases that never existed, and Amazon sold mushroom foraging guides that encouraged the picking of poisonous and protected fungi because the authors took AI suggestions at face value without verifying the facts. AI should never be the only source you use when searching for information; always double-check with primary sources produced by human experts.

Con: Bias in AI Training Data

AI models are trained on data from their users and the internet, which can introduce biases in their responses. If enough people think that pineapple on pizza is the best way to prepare the dish, then the AI chatbot may recommend it when you ask what the best type of pizza is (even when it's objectively wrong). Responses from ChatGPT should not be considered extensive deep dives on a subject, but more of an overview or user consensus that can inspire further exploration.

Con: Ethical and Privacy Concerns

There are serious privacy and ethical concerns with ChatGPT. You should never share your data with any of these models. They store every piece of information that's been given and can be reverse-engineered to spit out that information to strangers. There are also ethical concerns regarding AI taking jobs away from creatives and programmers, because some oligarchs elect to use AI when doing so is cheaper or more cost-effective than retaining or hiring real people.

Bigger than Instagram

ChatGPT has exploded in popularity and has become one of the fastest-growing online tools. In the first five days of its launch in 2023, ChatGPT reached over five million users, and two months later, it had over 100 million. It took Instagram and Facebook four years to hit that same number of users.

There's no denying that ChatGPT has fundamentally changed the digital landscape practically overnight. It is one of the ten most visited websites, getting approximately 5.2 billion visits per month and processing over one billion queries a day. According to the Pew Research Center, 23 percent of all U.S. adults have used the website, and about a quarter of teens use ChatGPT for schoolwork. Though Facebook and Google still have the largest user bases, it's clear that ChatGPT could catch up to them in just a few years.

And the website is only growing. In March 2025, the company behind ChatGPT, OpenAI, raised $40 billion in the largest funding round for a tech company ever, bringing its valuation to $350 billion. That makes it one of the highest-valued tech companies in the world, and it still hasn't hit the ceiling.

Tech companies in general tend to be overvalued compared to their actual worth, with venture capitalists chucking as much money as possible at the next shiny thing to get in on the bottom floor. But as long as ChatGPT remains a practical resource that doesn't become worse over time, it will remain highly valuable and incredibly popular.

THE FUTURE OF CHATGPT IN EVERYDAY LIFE

When you see the headlines around ChatGPT's massive growth and revenue, it can be easy to assume that the technology isn't meant for the average person. Just a decade ago, this proprietary technology would have been trapped behind a massive paywall that only the richest companies could ever afford.

But ChatGPT and other AI programs aren't just a moneymaking tech trend for entrepreneurs. Though these websites can help large Fortune 500 companies do a lot of large-scale work that replaces workers they feel can be automated, that isn't where the website shows off its full potential. ChatGPT is at its best when it's helping you solve little problems in ways that can improve your everyday life.

Why ChatGPT Makes a Great Personal Assistant

A personal assistant used to be a luxury for those who could afford to pay a real person to help set up their schedule, do chores, or turn their ideas into actionable plans. Though ChatGPT will never be able to pick up your laundry or grab your coffee, there's plenty the app can do to help improve your everyday life.

ChatGPT is great at time management. It can schedule, make tasks for your calendar app, or create to-do lists. It can set reminders, structure your workdays, and even arrange get-togethers with your friends. It's also available 24/7, using its broad knowledge base to solve problems. It also won't judge you, no matter how ridiculous or silly your questions may be.

How ChatGPT Learns from You

When you use ChatGPT with a logged-in account or a long session, the app will learn from you and change its answers to fit your needs. You can feed it instructions (like remembering your name or an important date), and it can draw from that information in its responses to later queries. It's highly customizable; you can set up your goals or whether you'd like responses to be more professional or casual.

You can even upload documents that can be used as templates for future projects. The more you use ChatGPT, the more personalized it becomes. Save successful prompts for later, and if you use those prompts frequently enough, ChatGPT will be able to recognize what you want before you even input it.

Unlike a traditional search engine or a website browser, ChatGPT changes based on your inputs. It evolves alongside you, a partner that might make you forget it's just a bunch of code in a box hundreds of miles away.

The Impact of AI on the Climate

Though ChatGPT has a lot of positives, there are quite a few downsides, including the serious effect its usage has on energy consumption.

The servers that power ChatGPT are housed in data centers located all around the world. These centers are temperature-controlled and use large quantities of water for cooling, causing them to use a lot of energy. As more people use ChatGPT and similar programs, the electricity demand by these data centers will siphon off even more energy. It has been estimated that by 2030 data centers will use twice as much energy as they do now.

According to a 2021 paper by scientists from Google and the University of California, Berkeley, training one AI model used enough electricity to power about 120 average U.S. homes for a year. And using it needs even more power: "The average query uses about 0.34 watt-hours, about what an oven would use in a little over one second, or a high-efficiency light bulb would use in a couple of minutes," according to the CEO of OpenAI, Sam Altman, in a June 2025 blog post.

The carbon footprint of data centers is massive and growing more every year. But there is a push for more energy-efficient AI models, with the technology getting better over time. We can start using renewable energy sources that can mitigate the damage all this consumption is doing to the planet. In fact, many tech companies have begun exploring building their own nuclear power plants because of their high-output, zero-emissions energy.

THE DIFFERENCE BETWEEN CHATGPT AND OTHER AI MODELS

ChatGPT may have the best name recognition, but it's far from the only AI chat model on the market. Every week, it seems like there's a fresh contender that changes the formula, user interface, or functionality. There's Claude, which excels at incredibly complex reasoning; Gemini, which can interact with multiple models; and Grok, which is a news and culture curation bot for social media. Though each chatbot has its strengths and weaknesses, we still recommend ChatGPT, because it's the most popular and is constantly evolving. Every new model offers a leap in technological evolution, so you'll never feel left behind in the AI revolution. Though you should feel free to test the other options, be warned that some of the skills taught here may not work as well or at all on the other models.

ChatGPT vs. Claude

Claude was created by Anthropic in 2023 and has become one of ChatGPT's main competitors. Like all AI models, it is trained on vast datasets from the internet, which can result in biases or hallucinations. These biases may lead a chatbot to give you skewed, imbalanced, or even incorrect information, which is why you must assess all AI-generated content before using or sharing it.

ChatGPT vs. Gemini

New chat models are constantly being released, and Gemini is at the forefront of innovation. Gemini was created by technology juggernaut Google and offers answers pulled from the company's massive trove of information. If it's on Google Search, Gemini can find it. The innovative chatbot can also create realistic videos that are years ahead of the competition. You can access Gemini through your computer or download it as an app for your phone.

ChatGPT vs. Grok

Grok is the cursed gremlin chatbot available on Elon Musk's X. It is most commonly used as a real-time fact-checking tool on X, although recent iterations have included image and video creation. It has been known to share wildly inaccurate misinformation (including its opinion on South African apartheid) but tends to be more up-to-date on news and trends than other models. It is also willing to engage in more provocative discussions than other chatbots.

When using a chatbot, you should always be aware of what problems dependency on AI can cause. Make sure that you maintain control over your critical thinking and ethical standards, double-checking your sources on other search engines or websites.

hey

ask me anything

Chapter 2

Best Practices for Using ChatGPT

Unlike search engines such as Google that are fueled by finding keywords on websites, AI chatbots are designed to think through an answer creatively, so they need a bit more than words and key phrases. They need context. This is where prompts come into play.

Prompts, which are the messages you send to ChatGPT, should be direct and conversational, like you are chatting with a friend. There's no need to be overly polite when asking. ChatGPT is most effective when your prompts are direct and include a few key components. Here we will teach you some best practices so that you can understand how to make your own prompts and use the hundreds of prompts at your disposal in part 2.

WHAT ARE PROMPTS AND WHY DO THEY MATTER?

A *prompt* is an instruction or input that guides a model toward a desired answer. It can be a question, a command, or even just a topic, but it should be direct, clear, and specific. Because chatbots are more focused on the wording of the question than just its nouns, being as precise as possible will help you achieve the desired outcome. Communicating with a chatbot can be easy, but getting it to understand exactly what you want requires a bit more effort.

For maximum success using chatbots, it is crucial to fine-tune and engineer your prompts. Say you want lunch. Telling ChatGPT "make me a sandwich" won't get you very far. But if you elaborate, adding that you are a Michelin-star chef with specific ingredients and a time limit, it will produce a recipe that you'll be happy to try. You may have to enter a few prompts before you get exactly what you want, refining with each input. You might want to see what changes if you add olives or if you want to use a grill instead of a stove. Those little details separate the prompting pros from the prompting amateurs.

The most effective prompt is made up of six parts: task, content, examples, role, format, and tone. You don't need to use all of these for every task, but these aspects help narrow ChatGPT's guidance to exactly what you are looking for, cutting down on confusion.

Task

A *task* is the core of a prompt and gives the chatbot a direction on where to go. This is the most important and absolutely mandatory part of a prompt. You should try to start a task sentence with an action verb such as "generate," "write," or "analyze" and share what the end goal is. It could be one task, like asking to create a workout routine, or a whole slew of tasks, like creating a multistep program to fight foot fungus. Without a task, the chatbot has no idea what it's supposed to do, so make sure your prompt contains this essential component. It's important to experiment and figure out how to word tasks for the best results.

Context

Right behind the task is the *context* of your prompt. It's the added information that makes the prompt more specific, adding layers and nuance that will improve ChatGPT's chance of arriving at the right answer. Theoretically, there's a nearly infinite amount of context you can add to a prompt, so it can be hard to perfectly pin down. It's helpful to add the background of the user asking, what success looks like, and the circumstances behind the need. The more personalized and specific your prompt is, the better results you'll have.

Instead of just asking ChatGPT how to plan a garden, include your level of expertise, what vegetables you like, what region you live in, and during what time of year you will be planting.

Examples

Examples will make your prompt better; that's just a fact. Including in the prompt clear instructions about how you want the answer outputted will help the chatbot understand what you are trying to say and save you some headaches when trying to refine it. You can use examples to help point it in the right direction. If you want ChatGPT to respond to emails or texts well, including a formula or script that it could plug new information into will give it a structure that it knows how to follow. Examples are not as important as a task or context, but they will make your prompting that much better.

Role

Why not let ChatGPT role-play a bit? Asking it to be a teacher could help with study prep, and instructing it to pretend to be a coach might result in some personalized workout routines. When writing a prompt, ask yourself who you want ChatGPT to be and why they'd be able to help you. You can even ask for specific individuals, but unless they are super famous, these requests may not change the results. ChatGPT is going to have a good understanding of how Einstein might help you with your science homework, but it may not have enough knowledge about your friend Craig to effectively mimic his suggestions for you.

Format

You can create a prompt from any combination of words in the English language, but it helps if ChatGPT can understand them. Using a recognizable, or even repeatable, format will help keep your prompts clean and give you the answers you are looking for. You can have answers created in the form of spreadsheets or tables or exported to other apps. Even if you wouldn't have the time or energy to do it yourself, ChatGPT can take the data that you give it and create something legible that saves you time. I've found it useful to ask ChatGPT to organize feedback I've received, telling it to break the paragraphs up into individual headers.

Tone

As in conversation with real people, tone is important when conveying what you are trying to say. You can have ChatGPT tell you an answer with any type of mood or tone. It can give you the weather optimistically, respectfully write an email, or begrudgingly send a birthday message to an ex-partner. Feel free to search for different mood words online, because there's no way you'll remember every synonym for *happy* that's in the dictionary.

The actual tone in which you write the message can also help your prompting. Yelling or screaming at the chatbot, using capital letters to convey anger or a need to hurry, won't give you a better answer. It might help you cool down a bit, since you can yell at a chatbot and not feel like you are abusing someone, but it won't improve your prompts.

OPEN-ENDED VS. SPECIFIC PROMPTS

When writing prompts, it's important to be as specific as possible. Writing an open-ended prompt will give you an answer, but it will most likely be vaguer than one written with more specific language. Here's a prompt that can seem simple, but the added language can make it shine.

Example: Finding a Restaurant

OPEN-ENDED PROMPT

"What's a good restaurant to eat at in New York City?"

Why it's open-ended:

It forces ChatGPT to look through thousands of restaurants and come up with an answer. There are quite a few factors, including cost, type of food, and overall rating, that could heavily impact where you'd want to eat. But if you are trying to be spontaneous or just brainstorming, then this prompt is perfect.

SPECIFIC PROMPT

"I'm planning a day trip to New York City with three adventurous friends in August, and I'm looking for an Italian restaurant with outdoor seating that won't be too crowded. Create a bulleted list of five amazing restaurants in Manhattan and Brooklyn that are budget-friendly and offer gluten-free options."

Why it's specific:

It provides a format (bulleted list), a task (finding a restaurant), a tone (amazing), and a context (they are adventurous). Not only does it define the type of restaurant you are looking for, but it also ensures a more tailored response that directly answers your needs. It's more useful when you need precise, actionable results.

Ethical and Responsible Usage

In the same way a knife can be used responsibly or maliciously depending on who holds it, so can ChatGPT. ChatGPT is a powerful tool that needs to be used responsibly. It's easy to have a chatbot start doing things in your life that may not be very ethical or responsible.

If you have a high-stakes decision that could change the course of your entire life, like deciding where to go to college or whether you should take out a mortgage, there's no reason to trust that outcome completely to a chatbot. Your intuition and decision-making should always come before what a chatbot thinks. One of the worst things you can do is rely on a chatbot for every decision in your life, because soon you won't be able to do anything yourself.

No matter what, you should always fact-check information that ChatGPT gives you since it may not be right.

You should also not give ChatGPT any sensitive information, like passwords or bank account numbers. If you willingly input that info, others could maliciously coax it out of a chatbot and use it for nefarious purposes.

Also, if you are a student, it's a terrible idea to ask ChatGPT to write your homework or essays. Not only is detection technology improving every day, but you'll also lose the ability to think for yourself. Remember that after you graduate and in the decades ahead, companies will want to replace employees with AI whenever possible. The best safeguard against that is to develop the skills that set human beings apart from machines.

TROUBLESHOOTING RESPONSES

Prompting in ChatGPT isn't an exact science, and you may not get the answer you want on the first go-round. You might need to use different prompts or change your tone or words to try and elicit a better response. Just because you don't get it right at first doesn't mean that you are bad at ChatGPT; quite the opposite, actually. Even the best prompters need several tries to get an answer exactly where they want it, and they understand the key to success with ChatGPT lies in the give-and-take of prompts and responses.

Trial and error will be your friend when prompting, but I promise you'll get better if you follow our tips and keep working with the chatbot. This section is designed to help you work through responses to get the answer you are looking for.

Dealing with Vague or Inaccurate Answers

The most common flaw you'll find in a ChatGPT answer is that it is too vague or wrong. If you find yourself getting an answer that doesn't have enough meat or says the capital of New York is Buffalo, then it's time to reword the prompt. Try using more descriptive or detailed words; adding more depth to a prompt will make it much more reliable. You can also ask ChatGPT to clarify an answer, forcing it to rethink what it just spit out and potentially give you a better response.

Refining Prompts

If at first you don't succeed, refine and refine again. When looking to improve your prompts, you should always add more context and information. Make sure the prompts include most of the six parts described earlier in this chapter.

For example, say you use the prompt "Tell me about Sweden." That prompt may regurgitate what it sees on Wikipedia, but it won't give you exactly what you want to know about the country, because it's too vague, with no goal or context. Try adding an expert and a specific topic with a clear purpose, like "You are a Swedish tour guide. Tell me about the four best museums we need to visit over our five-day trip."

HOW CHATGPT CAN WORK FOR YOU

Now that we have the basics on how ChatGPT works, we can get to how you can use a chatbot to improve your life. A chatbot is fantastic at doing mundane tasks that require a lot of data entry or repetitive tasks. It can write emails for you to clients or colleagues, create a list of gift ideas based on a person's interests or budget, or even help organize a family trip by comparing flights, hotels, and attractions.

ChatGPT is reliable, accurate, and trustworthy, parsing through data and your prompts as effectively as your own assistant (as long as you make sure to double-check its work). It shouldn't be something to be feared or misunderstood. The headlines and hype make it seem much more complicated.

At the end of the day, ChatGPT is just a collection of information using your prompts and questions to give the best outcomes possible. It's just a machine meant to sound like a human, but without any of the creativity or empathy our species is sometimes known for.

ChatGPT on Your Phone

Originally, ChatGPT was available only through a browser on your computer, but OpenAI has released apps on both Android and iOS. These apps allow you to enter the same prompts on the go, syncing them up with your account so you can continue your conversation on mobile or the web. The app includes voice integration and allows you to take a picture with your phone camera and upload it directly to ChatGPT.

Apps on both devices are very similar, but Apple devices can interact with Siri and access your history offline, and they have haptic feedback (so they will vibrate). Also, Android tends to get updates at a slower pace than iOS.

Paid vs. Free

ChatGPT offers a free option but has paid premium options that offer various tiers of service (currently Plus, Pro, Business, and Enterprise). Subscribing to Plus, which costs $20 a month at the time of writing, gets you image generation, the ability to upload files, and access to the latest models. (Pro, which costs about ten times as much, offers even more advanced computing options you'll probably never need.) By playing around with both the free and paid versions, I found that the free option delivered when I just needed ChatGPT to answer simple prompts about selecting a restaurant or finding a gift to buy. For fancier prompts that interact with other apps or require multiple steps for setup, the paid version worked a bit better. Start with the free version to test prompts, and if you find that you want more in-depth or thought-out answers, it might be worth buying a premium version.

PART TWO

Sample Prompts

ChatGPT is all about prompts. Your words, tone, and sentence structure are all of the utmost importance when crafting prompts to instruct the chatbot. This is easier said than done, especially for people who don't write much beyond the occasional text or email. That's why this section includes more than five hundred pre-written prompts. These prompts are meant to be approached analytically, taking what we have here and tweaking them until they fit exactly what you need. Very little writing, but very big results.

The prompts in this chapter have more than enough information to guide ChatGPT to a solid answer. There are open-ended prompts that are simple and can be filled out to fit your specific needs. Then there are specific prompts, which use nouns and ideas that might need a bit more editing to give you the exact answer you want.

But the joy of the chatbot is that it rewards experimentation, allowing you to take these ideas to the next level. Try switching out the descriptive words that define tone, proper nouns, or the expert character you want it to portray. There's no perfect way to use ChatGPT, so remember to just have fun!

One final note, and it's an important one. Remember that ChatGPT is not a replacement for professional advice. If you have a medical, financial, legal, or mental health issue, you should discuss it with a professional. ChatGPT can help you have an informed conversation about such matters, but it can make mistakes, too. You should always take a step to verify its guidance is on track, especially if the consequences could be long-term or severe.

HOW CHATGPT CAN HELP WITH MEAL PLANNING

Figuring out what to cook for the week can be incredibly stressful. If only there were a device that could plan grocery lists, balance nutrition, and create delicious meal plans! Thankfully, ChatGPT is fantastic at creating structures, and you can use the chatbot to plan out every meal.

Before bringing a ChatGPT recipe to your next dinner party, I'd recommend testing it out a bit first. A chatbot doesn't have taste buds; it only combines piles of data to find something that fits all your criteria.

Here are a few prompts you can give ChatGPT to help with your meal planning and prep. These are designed to inspire a little back-and-forth about some of the most common questions.

OPEN-ENDED PROMPTS

What can I make to eat with the ingredients I have at home?

What are the most popular recipes people ask for?

How many calories are in my sandwich?

What's your favorite type of pasta?

What makes a balanced meal?

Give me some tips for making good eggs.

SPECIFIC PROMPTS

I'm planning meals for the upcoming week for a family of four, including two kids under ten. Can you create a balanced weekly meal plan with breakfast, lunch, and dinner ideas that are simple, nutritious, and kid-friendly?

I have a busy work schedule and limited time to cook during weekdays. Can you generate a weekly meal plan that includes quick, healthy dinners I can prepare in under thirty minutes, plus a shopping list for all ingredients?

As our family chef, create a weekly dinner plan that appeals to young kids. Include meals like macaroni and cheese, and chicken nuggets. Use a playful yet practical tone and provide simple notes or substitutions for picky eaters.

I'm planning a day at the park for my three friends and want to create a delicious and extravagant picnic basket. Can you generate a list of foods I can buy at the local supermarket that will fit inside an average-size cooler?

You are a professional nutritionist. Can you create a weekly meal plan for someone who is trying to lose weight, with meals that are under 500 calories each and high in protein? Include portion sizes and a corresponding grocery list.

Act as a sports nutritionist and build a high-protein weekly meal plan for someone training five times a week. Incorporate meals like quinoa bowls and Greek yogurt. Include three meals and two snacks per day, with an energetic, motivational tone.

You are Martha Stewart. I'm hosting friends for a cozy winter weekend. Build a three-day meal itinerary featuring warm, hearty dishes like stew and turkey. Keep the tone cozy and inviting.

As a world traveler, craft a weekly meal plan with dishes from different countries each day—like tacos on Tuesday, falafel on Wednesday, and sushi bowls on Friday. Include dish names and brief descriptions, and keep the tone adventurous and fun.

You are an astronaut meeting with aliens for the first time and want to show them the best food on planet Earth. Include a food from each part of the globe, making sure they complement each other. Use a sci-fi tone and present each recipe as part of a mission log.

I want to meal prep lunches for the workweek using affordable, healthy ingredients. Can you give me five simple meal-prep lunch ideas that store well in the refrigerator and are easy to pack and reheat?

You are a nutritionist with two decades of experience. Help me create a weekly meal prep plan for dinners that I can make in advance on Sunday. I want meals that last four to five days, are balanced, and can be stored in containers and reheated easily.

I want to prepare healthy lunches and snacks for the workweek in one day. Can you give me ideas for meals that are filling, easy to prep ahead, and packable for work?

You are my mother-in-law and are constantly picky about the food you get served. Make a meal plan I'll enjoy with inexpensive ingredients. Use a calm and soothing tone.

As a nutritionist who specializes in vegetarian diets, create a meal plan for me and my boyfriend for the next five days. Include dishes that use carrots, mushrooms, and tofu. Use a tone that's aggressive yet firm.

Act as my meal planning assistant and create a seven-day pescatarian meal plan with seafood and plant-based meals like grilled salmon and veggie stir-fries. Present it in a chart with breakfast, lunch, and dinner for each day. Keep it practical and easy to follow.

Act like my parents. I am a broke college student and have only have ramen, Easy Mac, and one can of beer. Give me a dinner recipe that will impress my girlfriend. Make sure to be kind and gentle with your tone and not too demanding.

You are an expert chef who has won multiple awards. Make me a meal plan for the next four days that will impress my family and friends. Avoid shellfish and cranberries since my husband is allergic.

You are an expert with an air fryer. Come up with the five best meals that I can cook in my air fryer for a family of four. Try to make them as healthy as possible with the least amount of GMOs. Use a playful yet stern tone.

Act as a certified nutritionist. I'm looking for an easy 500-calorie breakfast that is high in protein, but I hate eggs. Make me a chart that includes multiple recipe options that are nutritious and tasty. Use a commanding and assertive tone.

My fiancée is allergic to gluten, and I am trying to cook her a romantic dinner. As an expert chef, give me an appetizer, main course, and dessert that will impress her. Use a nonjudgmental tone.

You're a budget-conscious shopper. I need a five-day meal prep plan using just $50. Include a shopping list and daily meals with simple ingredients like rice, lentils, and oats. Keep it friendly and doable.

HOW CHATGPT CAN HELP WITH TRAVEL PLANNING

Planning your next getaway or vacation can be incredibly stressful. There are so many details to manage. Between choosing a destination, planning activities, and sticking to a budget, you almost need a vacation from planning a vacation.

ChatGPT is fantastic at figuring out these small details. It can work through a lot of the common (and not-so-common) questions you might have, although it does have its limits. It can't book your hotel or help set up flights, but it can find the best deals and places to go on your stay. Use prompts to teach it what you like to do—things like hiking or museum visits—and it will create a detailed itinerary that will help you have fun wherever you go.

Just make sure when using ChatGPT to plan your stay, you double-check all the information on other platforms. The chatbot might not be as up-to-date as Google or another search engine.

OPEN-ENDED PROMPTS

What's the best time to travel to Texas?

How do you deal with extreme heat when traveling to new places?

What makes a good airline?

What should I bring to entertain my toddler on a long flight?

What is the fastest form of travel to New Guinea?

What destinations are popular for people my age?

SPECIFIC PROMPTS

I'm planning a day trip to New York City with three adventurous friends in August, and I'm looking for an Italian restaurant with outdoor seating that won't be too crowded. Create a bulleted list of five amazing restaurants in Manhattan and Brooklyn that are budget-friendly and offer gluten-free options.

You're my travel planner. I'm going to Paris for five days and want to see highlights like the Eiffel Tower and the Louvre, and go on a Seine cruise. Create a daily itinerary with suggested times and places to eat. The tone should be excited and helpful.

Act as a budget travel expert. I'm planning a trip in August but have limited money to spend. Suggest five budget-friendly destinations in the Southern hemisphere and list the pros and cons of each. Be honest but encouraging.

You are an expert on writing lists. Help me create a categorized, printable checklist for an international trip, including documents, gear, and health-related items. Keep the tone clear and practical.

You are a local tour guide who has spent years guiding tourists through Tokyo. I'm in Tokyo and it's raining all day. Give me indoor options like museums, tea shops, or cultural experiences, categorized by how busy they will be. Keep the tone warm and resourceful.

You are the owner of a romantic hotel. Suggest three relaxing, beautiful destinations for a weekend trip, like a mountain cabin or a coastal town. Include highlights for each. Keep the tone thoughtful and cozy.

As my travel agent, come up with a detailed itinerary for a seven-day trip to Morocco for three people. Prioritize museums and places where we can buy handmade gifts. Give us a detailed list broken down by the hour, keeping the tone aggressive to keep us on schedule.

You are an eco-conscious scientist. Tell me which three vacation destinations have the lowest carbon footprint, most charming local experiences, and greenest accommodations. Give me a list of pros and cons for each location in a cheery tone.

You are Marie Kondo or a packing expert. I want to pack everything I need for a seven-day trip into a carry-on, including clothes and bathroom supplies. Give me a detailed, minimalist packing list with smart tips. Keep the tone clever and efficient.

Act as a travel agent who specializes in family trips to Orlando. Find the best deals on tickets to all Florida theme parks for a family of four for four days. Also, look for budget-friendly hotels near Disney World for four nights.

You are a wellness guru. Plan me a three-night retreat at a tropical spa where I can recharge, preferably with yoga, healthy food, and nature. The tone should be balanced and welcoming.

You are an expert at road trips around the United States and have a Southern accent. Plan me a route from New York to Dallas with enough rest stops, interesting roadside attractions, and hotels. Break it down on a list by hour and day.

Act as a veterinarian with experience dealing with pets on airplanes. How should I prepare my ninety-five-pound golden retriever for a flight from New York to Los Angeles, including what medication I can give him and how to calm him down? Use the authoritative tone of a professional.

You are an expert in solo travel who has been all over Europe by themself. I want to take a three-day trip to Venice but still feel safe. Plan me a trip that focuses on tourist areas and places with low crime rates. Be respectful and calm while walking me through a bullet-point itinerary.

You are just as terrified of flying as I am. Plan a detailed itinerary on how I would get from Boston to Seattle without taking a plane and using cars or trains if possible. Find the shortest route possible, calmly walking through each leg of the journey.

You only know unconventional forms of travel, like a hot-air balloon or a horse. Figure out how to get to New York from Boston and give me companies that can book my journey. Talk like a nineteenth-century explorer.

You are an expert in Brazilian culture. Plan a two-day trip to São Paulo during Carnival that lets me explore the city and its nightlife. Find the best restaurants or bars for English speakers. Use the tone of a local.

You absolutely love Detroit! What is the best time to visit the city to get the most culture, nightlife, and food? Make a pros and cons list for each season of the year.

Act as my last-minute trip planner. I have only two to three days to plan for a weekend escape and want to relax somewhere close. Recommend ideas like a golf course or charming towns with an easy drive.

I'm planning a girls' trip for my bachelorette party, and you are my bridesmaid. Where is a great place to spend a weekend with six of my closest friends to celebrate before the wedding? Keep in mind we have a limited budget, and I am allergic to shellfish. Keep the tone fun and playful.

HOW CHATGPT CAN HELP WITH FITNESS AND EXERCISE

Motivating yourself and preparing to get fit isn't easy, but ChatGPT can help. Your chatbot can easily set up workout schedules, create healthy meal plans, or design fitness routines to meet your goals. It can even help you stay on track, since it can be really difficult without someone (or something) holding you accountable.

My favorite way to use ChatGPT in the gym is as a progress tracker, logging my workouts and nutrition plans to keep me focused. I find that having a little voice that follows my journey with me makes losing weight just a bit easier.

While these prompts can set you up for success, they are not a substitute for professional advice (especially if you have preexisting health conditions). Even a chatbot designed for the gym cannot give you an in-depth analysis as good as a personal trainer or nutritionist would provide, but it can help you get started or keep you motivated once you have a plan in place.

OPEN-ENDED PROMPTS

What's the best treadmill for someone my age?

How can I build up my arm muscles?

Find me a delicious protein shake recipe.

Should I eat before or after I work out?

How can I motivate myself?

What's the healthiest meal for me right now?

How do I reduce soreness the day after a workout?

SPECIFIC PROMPTS

You're a certified personal trainer. My goal is to get fit at home with no equipment. Create a four-week beginner-friendly full-body workout plan in a weekly table. Include exercise names, sets, and reps that I can use three times a week in a supportive, motivating tone.

Act as a physical therapist. I'm recovering from a mild knee injury, but still want to stay active. Suggest safe, low-impact exercises for strength and cardio with modifications in a bulleted list. Include examples that will be easy on my joints, like swimming.

As a sports nutritionist, design a high-protein, 2,500-calorie meal plan for someone strength training five times a week. Include breakfast, lunch, dinner, and two snacks in a meal list. Use popular ingredients like chicken and eggs. Share this information in a motivating but stern tone.

Play the role of a fitness coach for busy professionals. I have twenty to thirty minutes per day and want to stay active. Create a list in a motivating tone with a weekly workout schedule packed with short but effective routines.

You're a running coach and I'm getting ready to run my first 5K in eight weeks. Provide a progressive plan in a bulleted list that includes walking and jogging intervals, rest days, and pace guidance. Give me motivation and notes to maximize my time.

Act as a mindset coach who can help me when I'm feeling discouraged in my fitness journey. Give me a pep talk and list five mental health tips to stay consistent. I want to feel like the small wins are worth something. Can you respond in a warm, uplifting, and inspiring tone?

You're an ergonomic health expert. Create ten 10-minute routines for someone sitting hunched over at a desk all day. Focus on the back, hips, and neck, and format them as steps with timings.

You're a fitness coach specializing in older women's health. Create a twice-a-week strength training program for women over forty looking to build strength and protect their bone health. In an empowering tone, provide a detailed workout routine in a list format.

Act as a fun family activity planner. Suggest five fitness ideas that parents and two toddlers can do together indoors or outside. With a playful and enthusiastic tone, create a short activity list that will keep these kids engaged and away from their iPads.

You are a fitness coach who specializes in helping clients lose weight. I'm trying to lose thirty pounds before my wedding in April. Can you create a daily workout routine with exercise names, sets, and rest periods? Be energetic and don't take any excuses when I'm being lazy.

You specialize in workouts for those who have to spend a lot of time traveling. I'll be on the road for two weeks with no access to a gym. Create a portable workout plan in weeklong schedule chunks, using resistance bands and my weight. Include examples in a flexible and reassuring tone.

I lift weights four times a week and want to improve flexibility and joint health. You're a mobility specialist who wants to help me on my journey. Give me a pre- and post-lift exercise formatted as a bulleted list with short descriptions.

Play the role of a gym coach who specializes in dealing with beginners. I just joined a gym and feel intimidated. Design a one-day-per-week beginner workout using common machines and free weights. Include example movements like leg press or dumbbell bench. Format as a workout list with a friendly and encouraging tone.

Can you create a schedule for me, with alarms and notifications, to remind me to drink water? Format as steps or habits I can follow easily each day.

You're a personal trainer with great taste in music. Recommend three workout playlists in a bulleted list for lifting, cardio, and stretching. Use example songs with title and artist in each. The songs should be high-energy for lifting and cardio and calm for stretching.

Act as a fitness trainer who specializes in couples' workouts. Create a fun fitness challenge that I can do with my wife that will test our strength but not cause us to fight. Keep the tone light and playful.

Play the role of a national park ranger who knows all the best hiking spots. Find the most challenging trail in the Northwest of the United States and plan a two-day route that will test my mettle and fortitude. Share a bulleted list in a no-nonsense tone.

You're a sleep coach for athletes. Suggest five tips in a list with brief explanations to improve sleep for better workout recovery. Include examples like sleep hygiene, wind-down routines, and supplements. Use a calming and informative tone.

Provide a detailed schedule in a bulleted list that I can use as a workout routine focusing on my arm muscles. Offer a mix of cardiovascular exercises, flexibility workouts, and recovery techniques. Provide beginner-friendly workout plans, along with guidance on proper form.

I want to become as strong as Batman. Design a workout routine that would make the Dark Knight sweat, complete with a nutritional plan and a bulleted hourly schedule. Respond as if you were Alfred, Batman's butler.

HOW CHATGPT CAN HELP WITH HOME ORGANIZATION

Life can easily devolve into chaos when nothing gets put away. Kids leave their toys out, dishes stack up in the sink, and laundry becomes an immovable pile. Staying organized and on top of things is hard, but ChatGPT can give you a system that keeps your life a bit tidier.

The chatbot is fantastic at creating schedules and lists, which can help you create a life that's free of clutter. It can also design a space-planning system, digitize your photos, or just give you the mental clarity needed to take on the day. Unlike a lot of tools and self-help books, ChatGPT can create a specific set of instructions designed to perfectly match your needs, without letting you get lost in the mess.

OPEN-ENDED PROMPTS

Where should I start cleaning?

Set up a rotating chore calendar.

What's the best furniture layout for my apartment?

What can I clean with vinegar?

Give me tips for decluttering.

How many plants are too many?

What's the most efficient way to organize my dishes?

SPECIFIC PROMPTS

As a professional home organizer, help me declutter my kitchen by creating a checklist to sort items into keep, donate, or toss categories. Include categories like expired spices or duplicate utensils formatted as a categorized bulleted list.

My closet is a cluttered nightmare. Help me create a system I can use to organize it into a much cleaner space. There are sweaters, shoes, baseball hats, and my third-grade middle school homework. Keep the tone nonjudgmental and don't make me feel like a hoarder.

In a clean and calming tone, design a closet organization system for a small wardrobe in an apartment. Suggest storage ideas like slim hangers, bins, and a seasonal rotation. Format as step-by-step instructions with tips for visual clarity and efficiency.

You're a house organizer with kids of your own. Create a kid-safe toy storage plan for a small apartment. Include ideas like labeled bins, underbed storage, and toy rotation. Use a playful, friendly tone and format as a simple guide with sections for daily, weekly, and seasonal organization.

You are a cleaning expert on the television show Hoarders. Give me a day-to-day schedule that will help me not get overwhelmed when cleaning out my grandma's overstuffed home. Include words of reassurance to keep me calm during this incredibly difficult experience.

Build a weekly cleaning and organization routine I can follow to stay on top of clutter. Include tasks for each day and examples like wiping counters or tidying entryways. Use a supportive tone. Format as a day-by-day schedule.

You are a chef who keeps your pantry beautifully organized at all times. Help me create a pantry inventory system to reduce wasted space. Include food items every chef should have at home, like grains, canned goods, and snacks. Format as a template I can fill in.

I've become overwhelmed by the thousands of pieces of paper I have in my house. In a numbered action plan and calm tone, create a system to sort and store papers like bills, medical records, and receipts. Also, give me a list of what I should digitally scan, keep, or throw away.

Act as a small-space design expert. Design an organized entryway for coats, bags, and shoes. Include wall hooks, trays, and a bench. Format as a visual layout with item descriptions and placement tips.

I have become overwhelmed with laundry and need a system that will keep it organized. We live in a five-person household, including three kids and a dog. Suggest solutions for washing every piece of clothing in a time-efficient manner and a schedule for getting everything washed.

Act as a family coach. Give me a three-step approach as simple bullet points for parents to help kids declutter their rooms without tantrums. Include examples like making it a game or giving them donation choices.

You're a Best Buy employee who has set up hundreds of home entertainment systems. I want to come up with a cable-management system underneath my television for all my cables. Use a visual layout to come up with the best way to keep my cable box, video game console, and streaming devices from getting tangled in a pile.

We have three cats at home and are struggling to find enough space for their food, water, and litter boxes so that they don't fight. Come up with a detailed visual plan for where the best place is to put all of their cat equipment, so they won't fight or be aggressive.

You are an expert in early childhood development. Come up with a chore plan for our family that has two five-year-old sons. Make it fun and exciting so that it won't overwhelm them and will keep them motivated.

I have ADD and struggle to clean my apartment. Come up with a bulleted checklist that will keep me motivated. Use positive, affirming language that will make sure I stay on task.

Act as a professional garage organizer. I want to transform my messy garage into a clean, functional space. Suggest sorting spaces for tools, seasonal items, and sports gear. Include wall-mounted storage and bins. Create a visual diagram that shows where everything goes in our twenty-by-twenty-foot space.

Our bathroom has become incredibly cluttered and gross. Come up with a schedule and plan of attack to wipe out the grime, mold, and mildew currently collecting in the shower and toilet. Act as a military sergeant who won't tolerate lazy behavior.

Act as a minimalist coach. Build me a simple, repeatable decluttering routine I can follow, formatted as a weekly task list. Include daily ten- to fifteen-minute tasks with examples like organizing a drawer or sorting mail.

My kitchen counters are always messy. Help me create a system to keep them clear, creating a tiered system for what appliances are most important to keep on the counter. Keep the tone strategic and format as a three-part strategy: declutter, relocate, reset.

You are Martha Stewart and are coming to my house for dinner. What are you looking for when judging if a home is too messy or cluttered? Give a detailed list of the things you'd notice and how it would be best to tidy them before you show up.

HOW CHATGPT CAN HELP WITH GARDENING AND INDOOR PLANTS

I do not have a green thumb and have killed almost every plant I've ever had. That's why I know it's important to have a system and rules when gardening or keeping your indoor plants alive. ChatGPT might not be able to physically put tomatoes in the ground, but it does know what the best time to plant them is and how you should care for them.

Gardening is a time-sensitive hobby, where one mistake early on can snowball into a disaster. Squirrels can rummage through your produce, bugs can eat away at your fruit, and bad soil can mean wilted plants. Keeping a proper schedule, where ChatGPT knows all the factors, will improve your garden. It doesn't matter if you are a newb with a trowel like me or if you've been mulching since you were a young kid. ChatGPT can help in some way. And remember, when taking ChatGPT's advice on living beings (even if they are just plants), you should always consult a second source or look for further research.

OPEN-ENDED PROMPTS

What plants grow best in Virginia?

How many cacti can I put in my planter?

What's the easiest vegetable to grow where I live?

What are the best plants for pollinators?

Set up a yearlong schedule for harvest.

How would you partition a garden?

SPECIFIC PROMPTS

Act as an expert gardener. I have a four-by-eight raised garden bed and want to grow vegetables this season. Suggest a planting layout for tomatoes, basil, and lettuce in a simple diagram and plant list.

I'm new to gardening and want to grow my food. As an experienced home gardener, help me plan a low-maintenance vegetable garden with raised beds, in a supportive and encouraging tone. Include five easy-to-grow vegetables or herbs, short care instructions, and layout tips in bullet points.

My tomato plant leaves are wilting and dying. As a master gardener, diagnose potential issues in a table with the cause, symptoms, and solutions. Use a nonjudgmental tone that won't make me feel bad for hurting my precious vegetables.

As an urban gardening expert, design a container pollinator garden with six plant suggestions, sun requirements, and container tips that will attract bees and butterflies to my small apartment balcony.

I'm starting to compost for my garden, but I don't know where to begin. As a composting expert, give me a bulleted list of tips and a guide on how to use compost properly. Keep it simple and don't get too overwhelmed with the stinky details.

I want to keep a gardening journal this year. In a reflective and creative tone, give me eight seasonal journal prompts that track progress, record changes, or inspire reflection. Present them as a list.

I'm growing vegetables in containers on my patio and want to make sure I have enough space. As a gardening-gear expert, recommend five essential tools for small-space gardening. For each tool, give a short description, why it's useful, and how to store it.

I want to stay on top of my garden all year. As an expert gardener, create a month-by-month checklist of key tasks (like pruning, fertilizing, or harvesting) that is straightforward and easy to understand. I live in the Northwest United States and have about eight by eight feet of dirt to plant in.

I'm trying to visualize what my four-by-four-foot garden could look like with optimal care and growth. Create a visual representation, labeling different plants and how far apart they need to be. Use an educational and holistic tone.

I'm just starting with houseplants. As an indoor gardening coach, recommend five beginner-friendly plants in a calm tone. Create a table with their names, light requirements, and watering frequency, and one helpful tip for each.

My indoor plants keep getting brown tips on their leaves. List a series of issues that could be causing this, like overwatering, poor humidity, or bad soil. Add their solutions in a bulleted list format. Be judgmental so I stop hurting my plants.

You are an expert tomato gardener. Give me step-by-step instructions in chart form on how to grow tomatoes from seeds. Break it down by week and include tips to help me grow the plumpest produce.

My plants keep getting too dry and they are wilting. Come up with a watering schedule, broken down by day, for three ferns and two cacti. Explain how to use a moisture meter and how to know when a plant is thirsty. Keep the tone fun and funky.

I have a one-by-two-foot planter in front of my window that I would like to grow herbs in. Come up with a detailed visual plan to maximize space in the planter. I want to grow basil, mint, and anything else there's room for.

Our living room doesn't get a lot of sunlight, but we still want to grow at least two different types of indoor plants. Come up with a bulleted list of plant types that would thrive in that environment, keeping the tone educational.

I want to stay consistent with caring for my houseplants. As an expert in keeping houseplants alive, create a weekly care checklist that includes watering, light rotation, pruning, and pest inspection.

I want to decorate my apartment using plants. Act as a home decor stylist and suggest five styling ideas with indoor plants like monstera or trailing ivy. Give a bulleted list with design concepts and ideal plants.

Act as a veterinarian and recommend beginner houseplants that are pet-safe. In a short table with a tone that's protective and practical, include safe plants alongside light and water needs.

I'm seeing tiny bugs in my plant soil. Act as a pest control guide and help me identify and treat common indoor pests. Format as a question-and-answer list in a calm, focused tone that reassures indoor plant owners.

I want to create a terrarium indoors, but I don't have a lot of time. Give me a detailed chart that shows me the easiest way to create an ecosystem that won't break the bank.

HOW CHATGPT CAN HELP WITH PET CARE

One of the greatest joys in life is taking care of a pet. But bringing another living thing into your home can add a lot more stress, and mess, than you were expecting. Whether it's a newborn kitten trying to claw everything in your house or a dog with an aversion to going outside, there are always new problems that need to be solved.

ChatGPT can't walk your dog or clean a litter box, but it can help solve issues, come up with planning regimens, or just give helpful advice. I just brought home a new kitten, and ChatGPT has been incredibly helpful in giving tips on how to get this rambunctious ball of energy to get along with my two older felines. Though it's a challenge, and you still have to put in the physical work, having something to ask with deep pet knowledge helps the process go a bit smoother.

Though ChatGPT might seem like it knows exactly what's going on with your pet, it should not be used as your only source. Consult a veterinarian or other professional if any serious problems arise.

OPEN-ENDED PROMPTS

What's the best time of day to clean my hamster's cage?

What is the healthiest food for my cat?

Is my fish sick?

How many ferrets are too many?

Do turtles make good pets?

When should my puppy be house-trained?

What kinds of tricks can I teach my parrot?

SPECIFIC PROMPTS

I'm bringing home a puppy for the first time. As a certified dog trainer, walk me through an easy-to-follow routine in a daily schedule for its first week. Include crate training, feeding, and socialization examples. Keep the tone patient, warm, and beginner-friendly.

My cat has been throwing up more hairballs than usual. Act as a veterinary nurse and list common symptoms with examples, like changes in eating or stress. Keep the tone serious, as I still plan to bring him to the vet.

I need help choosing the right toys for a high-energy parrot. As an exotic bird specialist, recommend several enrichment ideas and explain their benefits. Present it as a categorized shopping guide in an upbeat, practical tone.

As a pet nutritionist, explain how to transition a dog to a new food safely. Detail the process in a step-by-step format using an example timeline with breakdowns over seven to ten days.

You are an expert pet groomer who has handled Maine coon cat fur many times. Give me monthly grooming tips for that cat breed, including when I should brush them, give them a bath, and cut their nails. Format it as a care calendar and use a gentle, encouraging tone for nervous cat owners.

Help me set up a cozy enclosure for a pet guinea pig. Visualize a two-foot-by-two-foot space with bedding, hideouts, and toys. Break down by cost all the pieces inside in a warm and friendly tone.

Outline a checklist of essentials to pack for a road trip with my golden retriever. Include tips to calm them down in the car and how often we should be stopping at rest stops. Also, make a travel guide list of what items we should bring, including toys and water bottles.

I want to get my first fish tank, but I don't know which type of water to use. As an aquarium store salesperson, explain the positives and negatives of saltwater and freshwater tanks. Break down the costs of each, including maintenance and the actual fish.

Create a daily care chart for a senior dog with arthritis. As a senior pet specialist, include tasks like gentle walks, supplement timing, and joint massage. I'm going through a rough time, so make sure the tone is friendly, nonjudgmental, and inviting.

I want to start clicker training my ferret. As a behavior trainer for small animals, explain how to get started, what cues I should use, and how to apply positive reinforcement. Format it as a training journal entry with beginner notes and a daily schedule. Use a fun, playful, and supportive tone.

As someone who just adopted a three-legged rescue dog, I need a tailored care plan. You are a veterinary rehabilitation specialist and should suggest daily mobility exercises, mental enrichment ideas, and meal routines. Create a weeklong planner, broken down by morning, afternoon, and evening.

I've decided that I'm going to open a cat café and need to teach my employees how to take care of a dozen feisty felines. As a feline behaviorist, write a staff training memo covering body language cues, boundaries, and enrichment best practices. Include how many litter boxes and feeders we'd need and how often they'd have to be checked.

You're a TikTok-famous otter trainer. Draft a content plan for teaching otters fun tricks like going through tunnels and squeaking on command. Include props and treat suggestions. Present it as a creative storyboard outline in a tone that's playful and fast-paced.

I want to teach my two-year-old son how to best interact with our cat. You are a child psychologist. Come up with a lesson plan that we can use to help our kid get acquainted with our new pet. Make sure to include potential problems and solutions.

My wife and I are planning on adopting a chameleon. Come up with a bulleted list of everything we'd need to have, including cages, food, and humidity systems. Include a price breakdown of each and how much it costs to keep a chameleon in your home.

Our elderly dog needs to be put down, and I'm not sure how I am going to handle it. As a pet care specialist, come up with a detailed bulleted list to make sure that my dog has the most comfortable time before we bring him to the vet, including any things we should avoid.

I just adopted a high-energy herding breed and need help preventing destructive behavior. As a canine enrichment specialist, design a daylong schedule with puzzle toys, scent work, and off-leash training examples. Format it like a doggy day camp itinerary.

As a veterinary nutritionist, help me build a feeding plan for my adult dog. I want to include kibble, fresh food, and wet food to give him a diverse diet. Provide a sample seven-day rotation with serving tips formatted as a table in a practical, health-conscious tone.

You're a veterinary physiotherapist consulting for a retired service dog. Create a recovery road map with joint care and light exercise plans to help maintain mobility, with examples like underwater treadmills and gentle tug games.

Act as a working dog expert. I need a comparison of harnesses, leashes, and booties designed for mountain rescue dogs. Break them down by cost and popularity in a chart. Keep the tone technical and honest.

HOW CHATGPT CAN HELP WITH FINANCIAL PLANNING

As inflation rises and our pockets get lighter, making sure you are financially secure is a must. Having a set goal to reach, whether for a vacation or future retirement, will allow you to breathe easier.

ChatGPT is a unique tool for financial planning, allowing you to keep track of your expenses, bills, and payments automatically in one place. It can also be used to teach concepts like financial literacy, allowing you to save up cash and even invest in larger opportunities. I've already started using ChatGPT to help me come up with questions to ask my banker and accountant, so I know I won't get caught off guard during tax season.

ChatGPT should not have the final say in your financial matters. You shouldn't trust it to pick out stocks for you, spend your entire paycheck, or manage your 401(k). It is not a replacement for professional advice, just a tool to help you keep everything together.

OPEN-ENDED PROMPTS

How much money should I have saved by now?

Is it financially irresponsible to buy a boat?

Make me a financial planner that's easy to follow.

Can you organize these receipts?

What's the best way to save for a child's college tuition?

How much money should I put aside for taxes?

Is a 401(k) or a Roth IRA better for me?

SPECIFIC PROMPTS

I want to build a monthly budget I can stick to. As a personal finance coach, create a detailed budget plan based on a monthly income of $5,000 and monthly expenses of at least $3,000. Present in an educational tone and in a table format.

I've been struggling to pay off my $30,000 of credit card debt, and I think I need some structure. Provide me with a detailed plan that can help me pay off everything I owe in the next two years. Keep the tone upbeat and optimistic so I stay on track.

Act as a financial wellness educator and walk me through how to set up an emergency fund. Include examples on how to save and what emergencies I should plan for. In a step-by-step format, help me calculate the right amount based on my $3,200 monthly expenses.

I'm planning to get married next year. As a wedding planner, outline a savings strategy for a $60,000 wedding. Use examples like venue deposits, flowers, and backup funds. Format it as a monthly timeline.

I want to learn how to invest, but I'm overwhelmed. As a beginner-friendly investment adviser, explain key concepts like index funds, risk tolerance, and compound interest. Format it as a mini glossary in a tone that is simple, clear, and empowering.

You're a retirement planner helping me map out long-term savings goals. I'm thirty-five and want to retire at sixty-five. Based on $70,000 income, create a strategy using Roth IRAs, a 401(k), and other tools.

Help me understand my credit score. As a credit educator, in a friendly and judgment-free tone, break down what affects it, and explain how I can improve my score of 620.

Act as a finance coach specializing in resolving debts. I have three credit cards with varying balances and interest rates, ranging from 16 percent to 23 percent. Help me come up with a financial plan to cover the monthly minimum payments.

I'm trying to save for a home within three years. As a home-buying financial guide, outline a savings plan for a $40,000 down payment. Include examples of budgeting, side hustles, and investment options. Format as a three-year road map in a motivating and realistic tone.

My job is doing layoffs, and I want to be prepared if I get fired. As a financial planning coach, list the steps I should take, including creating an emergency fund and updating my résumé. Format as a checklist in an uplifting tone.

I run a small business selling duck key chains, and I'm having trouble organizing my inventory. In list format, come up with a system that will allow me to track all six different types of rubber ducks that I sell, how I can ship them, and how much money I need to set aside for taxes.

As a financial coach, come up with a bulleted list of tasks I can do to save money. Break it down by quarter and year, including examples like checking subscriptions and saving goals. The tone should be hard but stern, like an army general who needs results.

I've just started a new job with benefits. As an HR executive with decades of experience, help me understand what I should do with my paycheck. Include investment opportunities, taxes, and how much I should save for emergencies.

You are a money-saving specialist. I want to save $300 a month when I make $5,000 and my rent is $2,000. Come up with a bulleted plan to help me put this money aside. Include ways I could cut costs in a mature and mothering tone.

I want to teach my teenager about financial responsibility. As a family finance educator, create a weekly lesson plan on budgeting, saving, and smart spending. Include fun pictures and examples that today's kids would relate to.

You are a vacation planner who specializes in setting up budget trips. In nine months, I want to travel abroad to any country. Come up with a financial plan in a bulleted list, including how much money I need to put aside each month to save up for expenses.

As a financial literacy coach, help me pay off my $200,000 of student loan debt. I make $65,000 a year, and my monthly expenses are about $1,800. Come up with a plan that allows me to save money while also paying off my loans. Keep the tone light and fluffy, as this gives me anxiety.

We are expecting our first child and want to set up a college fund for them. Come up with a bulleted list of tasks we need to do to set it up, as well as what the best investing strategy would be.

I'm planning on buying some stocks, but I don't know where to start. In a chart form, give me a list of platforms I can use to invest in, with their pros and cons. Also, come up with a system I can use to save money, showing me how much it is proper to save a month.

I'm looking for a side hustle that can help me generate passive income. Come up with a list of five jobs I can do in my free time using the internet. Keep the tone educational and the jobs simple.

HOW CHATGPT CAN HELP WITH LANGUAGE LEARNING

For some people, learning a second language is incredibly simple. I've had friends who took three years of Spanish in middle school and are still fluent two decades later. But for the rest of us, cramming a whole new set of grammatical rules and words into our heads just doesn't come easily.

Move over, Duolingo. ChatGPT is great at helping new language learners as well as experts. The chatbot can help you learn vocabulary, understand grammar, and even practice conversations. I always hated taking language quizzes in school, but ChatGPT has managed to come up with a series of tests I don't mind taking while I try to teach myself Spanish.

OPEN-ENDED PROMPTS

Translate this English paragraph into Italian.

Teach me ten French words.

How do you order breakfast in Spanish?

What is the easiest language for me to learn?

How can I learn to read Chinese?

List some popular German idioms.

SPECIFIC PROMPTS

I am heading to Spain and want to make sure my Spanish is good enough. You are a Spanish tutor. In Spanish, and with an upbeat tone, write an itinerary of interesting places I should go.

Write a short beginner-level story in German about a dog who gets lost and add a vocabulary list at the end. Ask me three questions at the end in German about the story.

Let's role-play a conversation at a fancy French bakery. You're the cashier, and I'll order a coffee and croissant. Keep the conversation going by asking me about my background and if I'd like any changes. The tone should be light and bubbly.

I'm just starting to learn Italian. As a beginner language coach, teach me fifteen basic phrases for everyday situations like greetings, asking for directions, and ordering food. Create a table with the Italian phrase, English translation, and pronunciation tips.

As a teacher, I need help building a themed vocabulary set in French. To achieve this, create a numbered list of ten words related to "the weather," including their English translations and example sentences. Format it in a numbered list.

Act as a pronunciation coach to help me learn Mandarin pronunciation. Give me five example words with tone marks and describe how to pronounce each. In a detailed and encouraging tone, give me a bulleted list.

Create a five-day mini challenge to boost my vocabulary in Arabic. As a language coach, create five checklists that center on a daily theme, include eight to ten new words, and quiz me at the end. Tone should be structured and motivational.

Act as a daily language planner. Create a seven-day Korean study schedule that includes reading, writing, listening, and speaking practice. Include sample tasks like watching a K-drama scene or practicing grammar.

Pretend you are a Swedish mechanic, and I need to have my car fixed. Have a conversation with me in Swedish, asking about individual parts of the car and their costs. Keep the tone as organic to the source as possible.

I'm an intermediate learner and want to start thinking in German. Act as a language immersion coach and give me five training exercises with everyday prompts such as "Describe in German what you're doing right now" or "Narrate your thoughts in German."

Write me a quiz to test my knowledge of words in Hebrew. In a list format, include popular nouns like pets and cars. Then ask me in a loving tone how to translate them into English.

Act as a language exchange partner. Simulate a text conversation in Portuguese between me and a friend talking about weekend plans. Use casual language, contractions, and emojis.

Help me improve my listening skills in French. As a listening coach, recommend five beginner-friendly YouTube channels, podcasts, or songs. Include short descriptions of what they cover and what the best way to listen to them is.

You are an expert Spanish speaker. I want to improve my Spanish accent. Create a ten-minute daily routine that includes tongue twisters, vowel practice, and rhythm work. Use examples like "*tres tristes tigres*."

You're a flash card creator. Build me ten advanced vocabulary flash cards in Korean focused on emotions and personality. Include the Korean word, the English translation, an example sentence, and a pronunciation guide.

You're a memory coach for language learners. Help me memorize ten French verbs using mnemonic tricks or vivid imagery. Format it as a two-column table with the verb and its memory device in a tone that is fun and imaginative.

I want to test my Spanish reflexes. You're a language drill coach—quiz me with ten rapid-fire translation challenges from English to Spanish using common phrases. Format it as a call-and-response in a tone that's challenging, motivating, and fast-paced.

In a printable cheat sheet, build me a custom set of fifteen Spanish phrases related to ordering food. Include literal translations, common usage, and pronunciation.

You're a multilingual comedian. Teach me ten funny expressions or wordplay exercises in German that show off the language's quirky side. Format as a set list and talk in a playful and funny tone that would work in a comedy club.

Help me practice small talk in French. As a conversation coach, create three short dialogues: about the weather, weekend plans, and hobbies. Keep the responses in a question-and-answer format that's casual, polite, and socially confident.

HOW CHATGPT CAN HELP WITH ENTERTAINMENT AND CREATIVE WRITING

When you have a deadline or a story you want to tell, there's nothing worse than writer's block. Being stuck at the edge of your scene or your story can put an end to your project, but thankfully, ChatGPT can help pull you back. Treating the software like a writing partner allows you to brainstorm, bounce around ideas, and hopefully come out of your writing session with an entirely new way to think.

Though ChatGPT is incapable of actually being creative, it can mimic the same thought processes that allow us to get out of funks. As long as you use it as a tool and not a replacement for the work you want to create, it's absolutely worth giving it a shot.

ChatGPT can also be used as an entertainment tool. As long as you aren't taking things too seriously, you can pretend to have a chat with Abraham Lincoln, play chess with a robotic grandmaster, or just listen to it tell you what it thinks are hilarious knock-knock jokes.

OPEN-ENDED PROMPTS

What is a synonym for *fun*?

How would you fix this story?

Tell me ten jokes I could share at work.

Can you build a writing schedule to help me finish a novel?

What is my character's motivation?

How do you entertain yourself?

Make me an outline for a romantasy novel.

SPECIFIC PROMPTS

Create a character profile for Dungeons & Dragons about a retired monster hunter who now lives in a peaceful town. Include quirks, habits, and how they hide their past from neighbors. Make the tone witty but grounded.

Describe a fantasy setting where artificial intelligence has started to take over the world. With a dark and moody tone, give the story a beginning, middle, and end. Make sure that humanity wins in the end.

Come up with ten jokes I can tell at work to my guy friends as we stand around the watercooler. Keep the lines funny and topical, without getting too controversial or nasty. Keep them in a list broken up into setups and punch lines.

You are a professional book reviewer. The character in the thriller I'm writing is stuck at a crossroads. Help me spitball a few different ideas in a calm tone, starting from them leaving their house to ending up in a haunted mansion.

I've been working on this book for months, and I'm stuck. Write me an in-depth examination of my character's fears and weaknesses, broken down in a bulleted list. They are a sixteen-year-old girl who lives in Albuquerque, loves Labubus, and hates when traffic lights take too long.

Aliens land in your backyard, but instead of invading, they beg you to help them become TikTok famous. Write the first conversation you have with them, what dances you plan on doing, and how you plan their viral debut.

You wake up with the ability to hear plants talking, but only in passive-aggressive comments. Write a scene where your houseplants start airing their grievances about your care routine, your life choices, and that fake fern in the corner.

You are an expert video game player from the 1980s who has now grown old. An old video game cartridge from your childhood starts talking to you, and it knows more than it should. Write your reaction and the first clue it gives you to a mystery in your past.

You accidentally summon a demon, but instead of wanting to end the world, it just wants to help you finish your to-do list and organize your email inbox. Write a humorous scene where it helps you respond to an email from your boss and do your laundry.

Come up with ten different sentence-long writing prompts that I can use to jump-start a novel. Each story should include five characters or fewer, and the environments they are in should be whimsical. Create them in a chart that breaks down each aspect of the story into its own row.

You are an internet journalist writing an article about a popular YouTube creator. Come up with ten different questions to ask in a list format to discuss how they got started, how they make money, and where they see the internet going in five years. Keep the tone light and conversational.

You are a published fantasy author. Give me five different plots for stories you would work on. Don't be afraid to change genre or use an unconventional story angle. Provide the answers in a chart format, breaking down each plot into its characters, setting, and overall stakes.

Here's a scene I've written for my first novel. Can you rewrite the first three paragraphs in a different style that adds more suspense and drama? Give me three different interpretations, each with its own style and flair.

You are a famous media critic. Here is the first draft of my manuscript. Please review it. Use an aggressive and straight-to-the-point tone. I really need an opinion that isn't trying to be nice, so I can work on not getting my feelings hurt.

I'm really bored and have an hour to waste while waiting for my flight. Give me three ways to amuse myself. It can be something I look at, something in a restaurant, or just a puzzle to keep my brain occupied. Your tone should be energetic and engaging.

Help me create a character for my novel about a dentist who is getting a divorce. I want them to take the dentist out of his funk and help him start his new life. Give me five different character sheets, with their bios, looks, and overall demeanor.

For my next story, I want a world I would never have thought of. Come up with five different settings where a young protagonist could find themselves and become something new. In a bulleted list, keep the tone enigmatic and cheerful.

You are an expert in the ways people talk. Can you improve this dialogue to sound more natural between two old friends? Point out what lines feel like they aren't human or are just unnatural. Give me at least five different ways the dialogue can be improved.

I want to design a video game, but I don't know which type would be the most entertaining. You are a young schoolboy addicted to playing on your Nintendo Switch. Come up with five different games you'd love to play, keeping the tone childish and realistic.

I'm working on a short story about a salamander that escapes from a lab and gets lost in the wilderness. Come up with three different story ideas on how this salamander could find their way back home, what dangers they'd face along the way, and what they should ultimately learn.

HOW CHATGPT CAN HELP WITH DIY AND CRAFT PROJECTS

Crafting can be a great escape from the stresses of your life, but it doesn't always come easily. Whether it's a knitting pattern that just isn't coming out right or a color you can't quite get on your palette, all it takes is one wrong move to ruin an entire project. That's where ChatGPT can come in, figuring out solutions to your DIY needs without forcing you to comb Reddit or the internet as a whole.

It can also be great for coming up with crafting projects, taking the materials you have and turning them into something new and fun. This can be extra helpful when you have kids around the house with nothing to do. Unsure of how to improve your Popsicle-stick sculptures with the little ones? Let ChatGPT take inventory of everything you have, and it will come up with a system that your kids won't be able to get enough of.

OPEN-ENDED PROMPTS

What's a good craft for a rainy day?

What types of crafts would I be good at?

Where is the closest hobby store?

How do you get into painting?

What should I practice drawing first to learn the basics?

What are the most beginner-friendly crafts?

SPECIFIC PROMPTS

I have two five-year-old sons and need to come up with a craft that will entertain them for a few hours. Give me five different crafts I can make with regular household items. Keep the list in a bulleted format and the tone light and cheery.

I'm looking to find a craft that will help me unwind after a long, stressful day at work. Give me three hobbies I can start that will help me unwind. Break them down in a chart by price, time commitment, and skill involved.

You are an expert upcycler and artist. I want to turn a pair of old jeans into a beautiful new piece of art. How would you go about doing that? Give me the instructions in a numbered, detailed list that explains each step of the process, from cutting to sewing.

Help me come up with ideas for seasonal home decor. For each holiday or season, create a piece that represents it. Use only items from nature or my recycling bin. Create a sheet with sections for materials, the time it would take, and fun factors.

I want to get into miniature painting, but I don't know where to start. Create a visual chart that outlines the steps to get started, the associated costs, and the available miniature companies. Keep the tone light and informative.

Design a fabric flag I can create to represent my love for vampires. Come up with a catchy slogan, a single image, and a pattern I can replicate. Break down how much the materials would cost and how long it would take.

Help me crochet a scarf out of yarn. I want the colors to be blue and pink, with a length of about three feet. Calculate how much time it would take, what's the best stitching pattern, and how much the yarn would cost.

You are Martha Stewart. I want to throw a big banquet with a centerpiece at my table that I can craft. Come up with five different types of centerpieces, breaking them down in a list format by their strengths and weaknesses.

I've always wanted a tiny dollhouse but felt they were too expensive. You are an architect for tiny dolls and are building a doll-size town house. Come up with a bulleted list of materials, labor, and time it would take for an adult to put it all together.

Help me transform a glass bottle into a beautiful piece of sand art. Come up with a design and technique that I can put inside a glass soda bottle that I can keep forever. Keep the tone informative and well-intentioned.

I have a Dremel, hacksaw, and 3D printer. Suggest three creative DIY projects I could complete with them. I am an amateur crafter, have about two hours a week, and am interested in making giftable items.

I am halfway through making my first set of shelves out of spare lumber, and I'm stuck. The shelves keep ending up crooked when I glue them, and I have no idea how to make them straight. Come up with a step-by-step plan to fix my problem, sharing potential hurdles or problems I can face along the way.

I want to build a sculpture out of scrap metal, but I've never welded before. I have about six three-foot metal pipes, duct tape, and a blowtorch. Can I create a piece using these materials? If so, what's the best way to go about it?

My jewelry workspace is a mess. I work on a small desk, and my beads, tools, and findings are all jumbled together. Can you suggest some clever ways to organize my supplies so I can actually find what I need when I'm working?

We are planning a weekend DIY project with two young children, ages three and four. We have construction paper, pipe cleaners, and a bunch of dried pasta. Give us age-appropriate, safe, and fun project ideas that teach basic crafting or building skills while keeping the mess somewhat under control.

I'm making a handmade gift for someone important, but I'm stuck on what to make. She's a good friend I've known since middle school and loves Pokémon. I want to create something special that she can cherish without breaking the bank. Come up with five different craft ideas.

I just finished a DIY project, but I'm not totally happy with how it turned out. If I describe what I made, can you give me honest feedback and some ideas for how to improve it next time?

I've been thinking about selling some of the mugs I make. Can you provide a business plan that includes the cost of materials and labor, so I can determine if this would be a viable job for me?

I want to get into 3D printing, but I'm unsure which printer to buy. Can you recommend five amateur printers, listing them by cost and accessibility? Keep the tone stern and professional.

I've got a random mix of beads, wires, charms, and leftover clasps. Can you help me come up with three creative jewelry projects I can make using just what I have on hand, without buying anything new? Keep the tone inspirational and kind.

HOW CHATGPT CAN HELP WITH SHOPPING AND GIFTS

Finding that perfect gift for someone special can be quite difficult. Browsing through dozens of websites and articles to find the best air fryer or necklace can take way too much time, and it's becoming harder and harder to visit physical stores.

ChatGPT is an amazing tool for coming up with the perfect gift for someone special in your life. Whether it's figuring out a budget-friendly present or figuring out what you can make on your own, a chatbot is a fantastic helper. Plugging in all of your friends' hobbies, needs, or lifestyle choices allows the chatbot to come up with a profile and tailor a gift directly to them.

Though ChatGPT won't be able to tell if they'll regift or already have that toaster, it can make the most educated guess and point you directly to where you need to go to get it.

OPEN-ENDED PROMPTS

Where can I buy a scarf?

What's the best gift for a mother-in-law?

How much should I spend on a birthday gift?

What is a good gift for my niece?

What are some popular birthday traditions from around the world?

Are gift cards considered rude?

SPECIFIC PROMPTS

I want to shop smarter and avoid impulse buys. Help me create a list with checkboxes that I can refer to before I buy anything I might not need. It should help me stay focused on what I actually need and avoid purchases I'll regret.

I'm planning to shop for gifts soon, but I never know what to get people. I'm currently looking for a gift for my mother, who loves flashy objects and colored glass. Can you help me come up with meaningful gift ideas within a budget of $100?

You are an expert home shopper. Come up with a list of five essentials every house needs, including links to the best options I can purchase. Keep the tone professional and kind.

Provide a list of five different toys I can buy for a ten-year-old. Keep them under $50 and include a variety of options based on different interests, such as educational toys, creative arts and crafts, books, outdoor activities, tech gadgets, and games. Include tips on buying gifts for young children and how to tailor them to a child's personality.

You're a tech adviser. I'm trying to choose between three laptops for casual use and light video editing. Compare options from Dell, HP, and Apple with specs like RAM, battery life, and screen quality. Use a balanced, informed tone. Format as a comparison chart.

Act as a thoughtful gift expert. I need gift ideas under $30 for a holiday party with coworkers. Include fun and useful examples like fancy candles, board games, or gift cards. Use a festive, friendly tone and format as a bulleted list with prices and popularity.

I shop at Costco and want tips for smart bulk buying without waste. Create a checklist of items I can purchase at Costco right now that every house should have. Keep the recommendations up-to-date, breaking them down by shelf-stable items or freeze-worthy foods.

You are a thrift shopping expert. I'm new to secondhand shopping and want to know how to find quality clothes and home items. Give me tips I should follow and what I should be wary of. Format as a numbered list in a casual, confident tone.

I want to buy a piece of jewelry for my fiancée, but I don't know what is popular. Give me a chart with images of popular jewelry styles, broken down by their price, availability, and how shiny they are. Keep the tone casual, like you are a jewelry store clerk.

I'm going to be shopping for a bra for my teenage daughter, and I don't want to embarrass her. Come up with a plan to buy her a bra that won't make her uncomfortable, allows her to buy what she wants, and won't break the bank. Talk like an attendant at a mall kiosk.

I'm trying to buy a LEGO set for my grandson, but I'm getting a bit overwhelmed. What are the three best LEGO sets for little boys that I can buy online? He loves Star Wars and trucks.

Plan a themed shopping trip where I can buy everything I'd need for a new kitchen for under $500. Consider each item's purpose and how it would be best integrated into a kitchen. Also, give me stores I can visit and how long this shopping trip should take.

You are an expert in home aquariums. I'm looking to buy a gift for someone with a saltwater fish tank, but all of the fish seem so expensive. Come up with a list of five different fish species I can buy for under $50. Keep the tone nautical like you are a salty sailor.

Build a stock-up schedule for household basics like paper goods, pantry staples, and cleaning supplies. Organize items by frequency of use and preferred brands and include timing guidelines to avoid overbuying or running out.

Christmas is coming up next month, and I need to buy gifts in bulk. What's the easiest, most cost-effective, and fun way to buy enough gifts for a family of ten? I don't want any single person to get the same gift or to make anyone feel like they got something less.

My dad loves the Muppets, and I want to buy him a unique gift for his birthday. Come up with five different and specific options I can buy, ranging from cheapest to most expensive. Include links and stores. Talk like Kermit the Frog.

My family wants to get a new dog, but I don't want to adopt some random mutt. Can you come up with five different breeders within one hundred miles from whom I can buy a new puppy? Give me a list of top reviews, prioritizing options that are the most ethical.

I've seen a lot of different mugs I want to buy on the TikTok Shop, but I'm not sure if any of them are legit. Can you comb through videos online giving reviews of mugs and show me which ones actually look like what they are advertising? Keep the tone professional and simple.

You are a Los Angeles tour guide. I would like to support small businesses instead of buying everything on Amazon. What are five gift shops located in Los Angeles that I can visit that won't break the bank?

I'm looking to buy a new microphone, but I don't trust the reviews I see online. What are the three best options for a desktop mic that won't make me sound awful in Zoom meetings? Share in a bulleted list in a professional and relaxed tone.

HOW CHATGPT CAN HELP WITH ART AND IMAGES

If you have ChatGPT Pro or use the mobile app, you can generate images through app prompts. Though AI images are probably the most controversial aspect of using a chatbot, there are still moments when they can be useful. Whether it's a low-stakes floor plan or a way to help visualize a complicated project, chatbots are more than acceptable to use.

AI art needs a lot of hand-holding, and you should put in the most detailed description you can. It may take multiple attempts to get the exact image you want. If you need an important image made for a birthday, an anniversary, or a holiday, try finding a real artist who will do a better job.

OPEN-ENDED PROMPTS

Draw me a dinosaur.

Create a floor plan for my house.

Design a vase.

Make me a meme about coffee I can share at work.

Create a birthday clown.

Make the best-looking jewels you can.

SPECIFIC PROMPTS

Can you create a banner for a children's birthday party featuring the Power Rangers? Make the Green Ranger front and center, with Blue and Red right behind him. Make their poses dynamic and action-focused.

I'm working on a ten-gallon aquarium, and I'm trying to visualize where everything goes. Create a visualized rendering of fish, coral, and gravel I can put in the tank and how it could look. Use real plants and only one fake object, labeling each with a red arrow and line.

You are an expert painter. Design me a logo for my painting business, using red and blue paints to design a dragon and a knight. Keep the style simple and elegant, making sure that it can be easily replicated.

Design a card for my grandma's eightieth birthday. Include blue jays around the outer rim, with a mockingbird right in the center. Make sure it doesn't look too crowded, keeping the birds as the main focus.

I'm stuck on this last level in a video game, and I don't know where to find the boss. Create a visual map of the level, putting an X over where the boss should be. Also include a bulleted list of tips for defeating the boss, useful items, and ways to avoid damage.

Design an ad for my matcha business, sharing a 50 percent off sale we are having next week. Include a delicious matcha latte on the bottom, with a green swirl coming out of the cup and circling the outer frame. Keep a white circle in the center where we can write the details of our store.

I want to know if I look better in a sequined gown in blue or green. Can you create two dresses in each color on a slim mannequin? Keep the gowns elegant and regal, using lots of sparkly colors and flowing fabric.

Create an image of a robot pal who looks like a small child. Make it white and futuristic, with lasers on both arms. Make sure it looks cheery and optimistic, posed like a superhero ready to take down some bad guys.

Design a lampshade I can make at home with materials purchased at the local store. Give me a few variations of the lampshade, with a bulleted list of parts and how much all of it can cost.

I want to know what a golden retriever dog will look like in six years. Create an image of a twelve-year-old dog, using the average look of most dogs of that species at that age. Make the dog look happy with a ball in its mouth, ready to play.

What do aliens look like? Design an image of what extraterrestrial life looks like, making the picture as realistic as possible. Follow what scientists think, giving a written explanation as to why it looks that way.

Give me an image of a rainbow over a beautiful mountainside landscape. Keep the colors bright and vibrant, with the rainbow cascading over the tops of trees. Put a single mountain climber staring up at the rainbow.

Design a diamond ring that my fiancée would be happy to wear. Use bright gold and flawless diamonds, making it shine and sparkle. Showcase the ring on a woman's finger, keeping the style as realistic as possible.

Showcase three examples of a book cover with the title Social Media for Newbies. Make the colors yellow and black, with a cartoonish person looking dumbfounded on the cover. The text should be bright and eye-catching, with a space at the bottom for extra notes and the author's byline.

Create an image of what the world will look like in twenty years if we continue on exactly the same path. Show a modern city landscape during the daytime, with buildings and people. Keep it realistic and explain your decisions.

Design a YouTube thumbnail for my gardening business. The video is titled "Favorite Mulches" and includes five of my favorite types of mulch. Include a bright background, various types of mulch, and an image of me looking excited.

Give me an image of a delicious hot dog with mustard and sauerkraut. Put it on a white plate on a picnic table, with a delicious can of soda with a straw next to it. Make it at sunset, with the orange glow of twilight cascading over the bun.

I'm working on building a new desk, but I'm unsure what type of wood to use. Visualize different desks made of walnut, cedar, and oak. Create another set of images, breaking them down into parts, sharing the positives and negatives of each type.

Create an image of a dinosaur in the style of four famous painters. Keep the images to just one dinosaur, making it as simple as possible without losing its original style.

I want to design a superhero costume for me to wear as I travel around the city fighting crime. Design a spandex suit in red and black colors, including practical shoes and gloves. Also, add multiple pockets where I can keep snacks and self-defense equipment.

HOW CHATGPT CAN HELP WITH CAREERS AND CORRESPONDENCE

Finding a job isn't easy, especially when recruiters are using artificial intelligence to review résumés before even reading them. So why not use AI to improve your chances of getting that job interview? ChatGPT has been fed an untold amount of job-related content and can be a great tool to get you that next gig.

Whether it's feeding your résumé into the chatbot or having it act as a potential employer for interview prep, ChatGPT can help you get organized for the next step in your career. You shouldn't use it as a replacement for your work, having it make up a fake résumé or accomplishments, but rather as a helping hand to highlight the value you bring to the table.

OPEN-ENDED PROMPTS

Can you look at my résumé?

Can you conduct a mock interview to help me prepare for the job I want?

What job would be easy for me to get?

Can you create a job description based on what I do at work?

How can you help me during my workday?

Help me write this email asking for a raise.

How do I respond to this job offer and ask for more money?

SPECIFIC PROMPTS

Write a professional email following up after a job interview at an accounting firm. Include gratitude for the opportunity, a brief reminder of my qualifications, and my continued interest in the role. Keep the tone warm but formal and help highlight my enthusiasm without sounding too eager.

I am applying for jobs and need my résumé improved. Rewrite my résumé, highlighting my leadership experience, job performance, and college degree. Include as much information as possible on a single page to help me secure the gig.

You are my boss at the local supermarket. Have a conversation with me where I try to get a raise and more hours. Be confrontational and rude, just like the real thing, including questions that a real manager might also ask.

I'm preparing for a job interview at a local law firm and need some help. Give me ten sample questions that I might be asked and potential answers to each. Make them in a bulleted list with reasons behind each question and answer.

Can you rewrite the weak bullet points on my résumé so I get more interviews? For example, change "manage social media" to "increased TikTok following by 12 percent in six months." Give me three before-and-after examples and make the tone focused.

Speak like a professional résumé writer in a confident and honest tone. Make my job titles more impressive without lying. My past titles were generic, like "writer," but I had leadership responsibilities. Suggest five improved job titles that better reflect my role.

I'm having trouble dealing with a younger coworker and want to make them like me. Write an email to a Gen Z brand manager expressing how much you like their work and how you'd be open to the idea of collaboration. Keep the tone youthful but professional.

Act like an entrepreneurial career adviser. Translate my freelance graphic design experience into strong résumé bullet points. Highlight skills like branding, time management, and client collaboration. Write three bullet points for each piece of work I had.

My résumé currently looks cluttered. Could you please refine it, focusing on the layout, spacing, and grammar? Recommend a popular template I can use. Keep the tone practical and warm.

As a résumé language expert, help me reword outdated or passive language on my résumé. I want each sentence to start with a strong verb and clearly show impact. Rewrite three to five sample lines to be more modern and active.

You are a professional résumé strategist. Critique the structure of my résumé. Tell me if the order of sections makes sense for someone with five to seven years of experience. Suggest improvements based on best practices. Keep feedback clear and helpful.

Help me remove filler words and fluff from my résumé. I want every word to count. Identify common weak phrases and rewrite them to be tighter and more impactful. You are my editor and know how to keep my résumé sharp and direct.

Respond like a résumé designer with a decade of experience. Suggest ways to visually improve my résumé without using graphics that confuse automated systems. Recommend formatting tips that keep it clean and readable. Offer layout or template advice.

I'm trying to get a promotion at work. Can you help me write an email explaining to my superior why I deserve this and a raise, using professional language? Include my accomplishments, my desire to grow with the brand, and how devoted I am to coming in to the office.

Translate my experience as a home health aide into bullet points for a hospital job. Emphasize skills like monitoring vitals, assisting with mobility, and maintaining dignity in care. Be compassionate yet clinical.

I'm trying to get a job as a professional LEGO model builder. Tailor my résumé to this specific role, highlighting key professional work experience that would be useful. Give me three to four bullet points on what I should focus on in the interview.

My coworker is being a little too friendly, and I would like to create some distance. Help me write an email that I could send them that establishes boundaries and my needs. Keep the tone super professional. Also, give me tips on how to escalate the situation if they keep lollygagging at my desk.

Help me list certifications and licenses correctly on my résumé for a healthcare job. Include CPR, BLS, CNA, and others. Suggest formatting and placement. Act like a résumé coach familiar with clinical requirements.

I'm looking to transition out of being a full-time writer into a better-paying job. Come up with five different positions where I can use my skills and earn more money. Also, rewrite my résumé for each different job sector.

HOW CHATGPT CAN HELP WITH EDUCATION AND LEARNING NEW SKILLS

Most of us learn new skills with YouTube videos, social media accounts, or good old-fashioned books. But information curated by others can only get you so far, and that information may not pertain to the exact task you're trying to accomplish. Rather than flipping through how-to books to figure out how to stitch a puppet, I can have ChatGPT come up with a lesson plan that teaches me just the necessary skills.

These AI chatbots can be fantastic teachers, using their collection of knowledge to help you learn in the style that's most effective for you. It's tempting to simply ask ChatGPT what you want to know, but the AI has limitations when it comes to specifics. It works much better as a teaching tool. It won't be able to dump a new language or the scientific name of a hummingbird into your brain, but it will help you create the skills needed to retain that info. I've found it helpful when creating flash cards or bulleted lists of questions that help me study new subjects I need to learn quickly.

OPEN-ENDED PROMPTS

Help me come up with a lesson plan for my students.

What is the best way to learn a new skill?

Teach me the basics of coding.

What are some strategies for improving my SAT score?

How should I study for my final exam?

Teach me the history of the United States.

SPECIFIC PROMPTS

I want you to act as a travel guide and introduce me to the history of ancient Egypt. Break it down into three parts: daily life, major pharaohs, and most powerful deities. Keep it easy to follow, but add vivid details to make the learning memorable.

You are a world leader at a major summit. Help me understand the fundamentals of climate change by first listing the main causes, then the global impacts, and finally some potential solutions. Make it feel like I'm reading a short but powerful briefing in an intense but realistic tone.

Summarize the history of the Roman Empire in a timeline format, starting from its founding to its fall. Keep the timeline concise, but highlight key leaders, battles, and reforms. I want it to feel like I'm holding an excerpt from an encyclopedia for quick study.

Teach me the basics of astronomy in the form of a short dialogue between a curious child and an expert astronomer. Let the child ask simple, direct questions and have the expert answer with clarity and wonder, making the subject approachable and not too overwhelming.

I want to learn to speed-read, but I get overwhelmed by large walls of text. You are a reading coach creating a step-by-step routine that will help me learn scanning, skimming, and chunking. Keep the tone informational and fun.

Act like a guitar teacher giving me my very first lesson. Break it into three parts: how to hold the instrument, how to strum a simple chord, and how to practice daily. Make it so clear that I could follow along without already knowing how to hold a guitar.

You are an expert photographer. Help me learn the basics of photography with my phone camera. Begin by explaining composition, then lighting, then editing apps. Structure it as three easy tips that would instantly improve my photos, even if I know very little about cameras or artistic framing.

Teach me how to juggle three balls as an energetic, fun circus clown. Break the lesson into phases: tossing one ball, then two, then three. Include common mistakes and how to fix them.

Teach me how to code, using the most simplistic language possible. Talk me through the basics of coding, what the different languages are, and how computers can understand them. Give me the answers in a bulleted list, with subject heads and breaks between them.

Pretend you're a wilderness guide narrating a nature survival guidebook. Teach me how to build a fire, including visual descriptions of each step. Start with safety rules, then explain gathering wood, creating a base, lighting it, and finally, how to safely put it out.

You are a chess coach teaching me how to be better at the game. Come up with a bulleted list of skills, moves, and techniques that chess grandmasters use that I can replicate. Keep the tone serious as I train for a chess tournament.

Make me about thirty flash cards I can use to help me study for my Hebrew finals. On one side, put a basic word, and on the other, put the answer. Make it in a format that can be easily replicated, printed out, and placed in a pile.

You're a dance instructor teaching me a basic salsa step. In a visual format, describe the rhythm, where my feet go, and how to keep my body relaxed. Describe it in a way that even someone with no rhythm can use.

My mom just came back from the hospital with a broken leg, and I'm stuck taking care of her. Come up with a list of chores I should do for her around the house, and the best way I can take care of her. Keep the tone light and fluffy, as my mother is quite difficult.

Write a thirty-question quiz to help me ace my chemistry exam. The questions should be about atoms and how they lose or gain electrons. Come up with a separate sheet that contains all the answers and explanations for them.

I want to learn some skills that will help me remember tasks better. Come up with a detailed schedule of brainteasers I can do and when I should do them to help me retain knowledge. Act as a cartoon with immense energy who is beyond excited to help me learn.

Show me how to set up a simple budget. Start with listing income, subtracting fixed expenses, and creating categories for savings and leisure. Present it as a three-step system I could write on paper today, even without apps, so it doesn't feel overwhelming.

Act as a tutor. Figure out how well I know marine wildlife with ten different questions that test my knowledge. Based on my answers, come up with a two-week lesson plan I can use to learn even more. Include milestones, tasks, and resources I can use to fact-check.

Here's my solution to an algebra problem. Look it over and identify the wrong steps and how I can improve. Give me the answers in paragraph format in an educational tone. Also, give me a checklist of fixes I can use to prevent future mistakes.

Design a weekend project so I can learn the basics of knitting. Provide materials, step-by-step instructions, and helpful hints I'll need along the way. Present the project in a bulleted list with check marks that are easy to follow.

HOW CHATGPT CAN HELP WITH EXPLORING HOBBIES

Sitting in front of your computer all day can be incredibly boring, something most of us struggle with in our daily lives. Hobbies like knitting, painting, and cooking can give us something fun to focus on, but starting a new hobby, or even keeping up with an old one, can sometimes feel like too much work. ChatGPT can help.

Hobbies can be incredibly time-consuming or require certain skills that need to be learned. These are all things ChatGPT can help you structure and manage. You want to spend your time making a great scarf, not sifting through dozens of books or YouTube videos on how to get the perfect pattern.

I've found that ChatGPT can be a great tool to find the exact hobby you could get into. For example, I asked the chatbot how expensive and practical starting an herb box in an apartment would be, and it talked me out of wasting space on low-yielding basil. So instead, when I asked it for recommendations, it pointed me toward 3D printing, a hobby that's given me a nearly endless stream of plastic fidget toys.

OPEN-ENDED PROMPTS

What's a good hobby to start?

How do you get into knitting?

What's the easiest hobby?

Can you recommend some hobbies that aren't expensive?

What's the most popular hobbies for people my age?

Find me a hobby that keeps me away from the internet.

What's a low-effort hobby I can enjoy in an hour or less?

SPECIFIC PROMPTS

I want to start a hobby, but I don't know which one to pick. Provide me with five different hobbies and list their pros, cons, and associated expenses in a chart. Include mainstream popular options as well as more obscure hobbies I might find interesting.

You are an expert knitter with years of experience. Write me a guide on how to get started knitting, including all the basic tips, rules, and tools needed. Include sections on cost and the time required to create a clothing item. Keep the tone fun but informative.

My goal is to paint an entire army of miniatures to use in a game of Warhammer. Give me five different classes and create a list of the costs associated with creating an army. Keep the tone light but serious, as if you were an elf.

Act as an expert barista who teaches classes on coffee making. I recently bought an espresso machine and want to learn how best to use it. Come up with a bulleted chart that includes bean selection, extra equipment, and common mistakes when brewing.

Design a beginner's maker project to explore safety in woodworking. Specify required tools, materials, cuts, and step-by-step assembly. Add a photo checklist, sanding and finishing tips, and a five-minute daily practice routine.

You are an expert bird-watcher. Teach me the best skills to spot birds in New England. Include a list of necessary equipment and the best books for identifying birds. Create a mini field journal I can use to log my sightings.

Act as a teacher for smartphone filmmaking. Outline a weekend boot camp: storyboarding, shot types, lighting, sound, and editing. Provide a three-scene script, shot list, and timing guide. Include a peer review checklist and export settings for social platforms. Prioritize learning by doing.

Teach me to explore mushroom cultivation at home. Explain sterile technique, substrate choices, growth stages, and contamination troubleshooting. Provide a starter kit bill of materials, a setup diagram, and a daily care calendar. Keep the tone intense and straight to the point.

Act as an expert in astronomy, giving me a crash course on how to study the sky. Provide a detailed list of equipment and its cost. Share important apps and tips on how to best spot planets and stars.

Help me try lockpicking as a skill-building hobby. Recommend good beginner locks I should practice on and visuals on how best to take them apart. Include a weekly practice plan, troubleshooting tips, and links to competitions.

Plan a fermentation lab for learning to make kimchi. Provide ingredients, equipment, sanitation steps, salting ratios, and fermentation temperature guidance. Add a day-by-day timeline with checkpoints. Include a flavor-adjustment decision tree, storage safety, and ways to document results. Keep the tone serious.

I want to find a hobby I can do with my wife. Can you give me a list of three different hobbies that are good for couples? Can you break them down by cost, how much time you need to invest, and the skill level required? Know that we are both not very athletic or tactile.

You are a bonsai expert offering classes. Give me a detailed breakdown of what you'd tell students trying to grow, trim, and maintain their first tree. Include pruning rules, wiring basics, watering schedule, and light requirements.

Give me a detailed breakdown of creating a dragon out of origami. Use visual cues to show where I need to fold the paper and how thick it should be. Include error areas, estimated times, and how to avoid paper cuts.

Create a beginner's 3D-printing playbook. Recommend an entry-level printer, safety steps, filament choices, and bed preparation. Outline three training prints, like a calibration cube, phone stand, or articulated toy, with slicer settings, common failures, and fixes. Include a maintenance schedule and a checklist for post-processing: trimming, sanding, and optional painting.

I want to learn how to make house music without expensive gear. Give me a ten-week course that explains the basics of rhythm, the programs I can use, instruments, effects, and arrangements. Provide a one-page song template, reference track checklist, metronome drills, and a rough-mix workflow.

Teach me beginner card magic focused on sleight of hand. Outline a progressive routine: overhand control, false cut, key card, double lift, and an audience-ready trick. Include practice timers, misdirection principles, angles, and patter writing. Add a rehearsal checklist and filming guidelines to self-critique performance in a tone that is smooth and convincing.

Be my geocaching trail guide. Start with a quick safety and etiquette checklist, then pick three caches close to an urban park near me. Provide coordinates, hints, logging tips, and a photo scavenger list. Provide a log where I can input my findings.

Guide me through building a closed moss terrarium. Supply a materials checklist, layering order, jar sterilization tips, and water management. Schedule setup, first-week monitoring, and monthly trimming. Include a troubleshooting decision tree for mold or gnats, plus a photo log rubric tracking growth, humidity, and composition balance.

Help me design a board game I can use to impress my friends. Help me prototype a game that lasts twenty minutes: its themes, core loop, victory conditions, and budget for pieces. Provide a paper prototype, three playtest missions, data sheets for feedback, and a balancing checklist.

HOW CHATGPT CAN HELP WITH TIME MANAGEMENT AND PRODUCTIVITY

Keeping up with your busy schedule isn't easy. Thankfully, ChatGPT is great at helping people manage their time, tasks, and daily needs. It won't be able to magically teleport you to that dentist appointment right after a dance recital, but it can map out a way for you to stay on task.

ChatGPT can act like your own personal assistant that knows your schedule and what you need to get done each day. By feeding it information about what you must do, it can create a balanced schedule and explain how you can best use your time. It can generate printable charts and schedules, help set up calendar reminders on your phone, and teach you time management techniques that let you get more done in less time than you thought possible.

OPEN-ENDED PROMPTS

Create an hourly schedule for me for my workdays.

Find me the quickest way to handle my weekend chores.

How can I stay productive today?

Create a daily planner template.

What can I do to stay focused?

Give me a list of affirmations that will inspire me to stay productive.

SPECIFIC PROMPTS

I'm having trouble trying to focus on a work assignment that is due later today. Can you keep me on track by allowing me to use ChatGPT to look up information for my project only for the next hour? Send me an email when the timer is up.

Pretend you're my executive assistant. Build a calendar for next week, breaking it down by hour, with time for commuting and eating. Insert email windows, meal prep, and training. Provide a daily brief each morning and an evening audit with rescheduling recommendations.

Act as a focus therapist. Interview me to find distraction triggers and energy patterns. Prescribe environmental tweaks, notifications, and a two-tier to-do list for tasks that are critical or simply nice to have. Include a boredom plan, a recovery protocol after I screw up, and a self-compassion script for setbacks.

Help me build an anti-procrastination playbook. Identify common avoidance problems, friction points, and perfectionist traps. Prescribe tiny first steps, countdowns, temptations to avoid, and public commitments. Include a relapse worksheet, a momentum tracker, and a five-minute rescue routine for when motivation collapses completely.

I need a schedule to help make sure I have enough time to pick up my kids from school. Give me a daily reminder around 4 p.m. that I need to be in my car and ready to head to school to pick up my kids. Keep the tone light and refreshing but do whatever you can so I don't forget.

Act as my personal assistant, planning my daily routine. Read through all my emails sent the day before and summarize them into three bullet points. Include quick responses and flag any that seem urgent. Respond in a Southern dialect with whimsy and charm.

Design a short focus session. Outline one 25-minute task, three 3-minute stretches, then another 25-minute task. Add a simple note template to capture distractions. Include one motivation response and one small treat afterward. Keep directions straightforward so I can start immediately without overthinking.

Act as a reminder buddy. Every hour, ask if I'm still on the chosen task. If not, help me pick the next smallest step. Suggest one breathing exercise, one stretch, and one hydration option. Keep language short, supportive, and free of jargon.

Build a simple weekly plan. For each weekday, choose one task and two supporting actions. Reserve Friday afternoon for review and cleanup. Add two life tasks, like groceries or laundry. Provide a minimal calendar layout I can copy into my note app.

I find myself getting easily distracted by social media whenever I try to do work. Give me five ways I can keep myself focused on my task without having to download new programs or apps. Make sure they aren't boring or too difficult, as that will make me not want to use them.

My kids keep distracting me while I'm trying to work from home. Give me five different crafts or activities I can give them that will distract them for a few hours, so I don't get fired and can continue to pay rent.

Create a five-sentence email guide. Sentence one: Delete obvious clutter. Two: Archive newsletters. Three: Reply to anything in under two minutes. Four: Flag messages needing thought. Five: Schedule one block to handle flagged items. Keep it simple enough to use every morning.

I am planning a day out with my kids and need to schedule some activities. Come up with an hourly schedule of what we can do as a family, giving time for food, bathroom, and tantrum breaks. Keep the tone light and fun, as I expect to be incredibly stressed.

Write a tiny contract. I will start [task] at [time], work until the timer ends, and ignore other apps. If I get distracted, I will note it and restart. Afterward, I'll record one sentence about progress and what I need to do next.

As my personal assistant, come up with an hourly breakdown of what I need to get done today. Focus on the most important tasks, like picking the kids up from the pool or grabbing groceries. After I finish each task, give me a positive affirmation and remind me of a small treat I can have.

I'm tired of having to remind my husband to do the dishes. Come up with a daily task reminder that emails him at exactly 7 p.m. to get the dishes done.

Act as a professional time organizer. List five different systems I can use to make use of my time better. Break each into a bulleted list with pros, cons, skill ceiling, and time investment. Include YouTube videos or links so I can research further.

Act as a morning jump start. Ask me for today's three priorities, estimate durations, choose one starting task, and set a timer. Provide a single-sentence pep talk, two phone-distraction blockers, and a five-minute micro warm-up. Keep instructions short, friendly, and immediately actionable.

Design a distraction trapdoor. When I report a distraction, classify it, schedule it for later, and give me the tiniest next action on my current task. Provide a one-breath reset and restart the timer. Keep messages kind, direct, and free from motivational nonsense.

Act as a gentle interrupter. Every ninety minutes, ask what I'm doing, compare it to the plan, and help me recommit or pivot. Log one win and one obstacle. Suggest one micro-break and a treat I can eat.

HOW CHATGPT CAN HELP WITH PARENTING AND FAMILY ADVICE

Being a parent can be incredibly stressful, with new problems and new worries seeming to pop up every day. There's a lot to keep track of regardless of what age your kids are right now. Parents of teens are struggling with attitude and emotions, huge grocery bills, and the financial stress of college or just them moving out on their own on the horizon. Parents with newborns are worried about enrichment and choices, making sure they're doing what's best for their baby. And for all the parents with children in between there's plenty to figure out, such as school, screen time, and healthy habits.

ChatGPT can help with this. At the very least it can be a useful sounding board for parents to vent and problem-solve, but it can provide proactive tips too. While it should never be a replacement for pediatricians or therapists, ChatGPT can help parents brainstorm with purpose in those moments when they're too tired or too frustrated to figure out what to do next.

OPEN-ENDED PROMPTS

How long should my kid be on their iPad?

What parks and playgrounds are open within thirty minutes of where I live?

Help me with my child's homework.

How can I fix a picky eater?

I need help figuring out how to talk to my kid at the end of the day.

Why is my baby waking up so much?

SPECIFIC PROMPTS

My eight-year-old son just came home and said some very crass things about women he heard at school. What's the best way I can teach him how to respect women? Include examples of conversations, including his responses, in an educational tone.

Act as a family coach. Build a morning routine for my four-year-old daughter. She struggles with getting dressed and taking instructions. Give me three steps I can take, including positive reinforcement. Make the list printable so I can put it on the refrigerator.

You are a children's book author. Write a four-hundred-word bedtime story that includes morals about bravery, helping others, and friendship. The child loves owls, dinosaurs, and staying up past their bedtime. Output the sections in a title, story, theme, and questions.

Build a calm-down plan for after-school meltdowns. Triggers are noise and hunger. Provide a five-minute sequence including sensory options, movement, hydration, and a script. Add a backpack-ready kit list. As a pediatrician, include a bulleted guide in a soft tone.

Compose a weekly parenting sync agenda for co-parents in alternating households. Include sections on wins, challenges, schedules, shared rules, handoff checklist, and upcoming decisions. Add a respectful template message for disagreements and a child-facing summary.

My grandma won't stop talking about controversial topics at the dinner table. Create a bulleted list of talking points I can bring up at dinner whenever she tries to rant. Keep the topics light, topical, and away from all politics.

You are an internet security expert. Help me come up with a plan to keep my six-year-old safe online. Come up with a list of child-safe apps I can download on their iPad, as well as ways I can block harmful content on apps like YouTube and iMessage.

My kids will not share any of their toys. Come up with a solid plan I can use whenever my kids refuse to share. Come up with three different ways I can save my sanity, using tried methods popular with child psychiatrists. Create a list of pros and cons for each.

We are trying to determine which family members and friends to invite to our son's first birthday party. What is genuinely a normal person that gets invited to a gathering like this, and who should we avoid inviting at all costs?

Create an age-smart screen plan for siblings eight and twelve using a Nintendo Switch and tablets. Create a bulleted list outlining the duration we should allow for screens on school days and weekends. Come up with a plan for if they need to be repaired, what exceptions we should allow, and how we can block inappropriate content.

You are a childhood psychologist. Create five concise scripts for ending playground time with a strong-willed six-year-old. Each should have a ten-minute cooldown, a three-minute warning, and a statement with empathy. Output them in numbered lines with likely child replies and brief follow-ups.

Plan a chore chart for a family of four with two fourteen-year-old girls. Include space for chores like cleaning rooms, doing laundry, and doing the dishes. Use colorful language and include spots for star stickers.

Write an email to a fourth-grade teacher requesting a meeting about the homework she's giving out. In a stern but light tone, share that you disapprove of the math problems being given because they almost always have to do with Bluey. The length should be about 150 words and should include a subject line and body.

Construct a bedtime wind-down for a three-year-old with separation anxiety that I can share with a babysitter or other caregivers. Include a warm bath, pajamas, two picture books, a snuggle, a lullaby, and lights-out. Add a door-check plan at five and ten minutes.

Draft a travel survival plan for a three-hour train ride with a spirited four-year-old. Specify seat choice, snack rotation, six activities, bathroom timing, and screen-time strategy. Provide two calming scripts and a meltdown protocol. Format a timeline and packing list.

You are a professional storyteller. Come up with a two-hundred-word story about a bunny who refuses to eat his vegetables but realizes how important nutrition is. Keep the sentences short and the tone jovial and cheery.

Design a reward system to keep my kids engaged. Come up with tiered rewards, starting from extra television time to packs of Pokémon cards. Create a system of rules that are beginner-friendly in a neutral and specific tone.

My kids can't stop fighting over toys. Come up with a simple yet elegant solution to keep my two sons from ripping themselves apart that isn't just buying new toys. Act as a parenting coach and use a strict but supportive tone.

Come up with an email form I can use to send to my kids' teacher about after-school studies. Include pleasantries and questions about what my kid can do after the school bell rings. Ask about extracurricular activities and how much all of them would cost.

My son will not stop pretending he is Batman. Come up with a two-hundred-word letter from the Joker telling Batman that if he doesn't finish his homework or eat his vegetables, bad things will happen in Gotham. Keep the tone playful and fun, like you are the Joker from the 1960s Batman television show.

HOW CHATGPT CAN HELP WITH MENTAL HEALTH AND MINDFULNESS

The world can feel complex and overwhelming, even during good times. If you need help finding your center or peace of mind, ChatGPT can help. Whether it's finding room in your schedule for personal time or having something to bounce ideas off, a chatbot can be immensely helpful.

Using it as a wellness tool, you'll be able to solve problems and look at solutions in new ways. It's great at helping you break the monotony of a stress-induced day or find positive affirmations to help keep yourself grounded. It's not going to make all your problems vanish into thin air, but it will at least help you handle the load of living in the modern world.

Keep in mind that ChatGPT should never be a replacement for a doctor or a mental health professional. If you are genuinely in a bad place or at risk of harm, turn off the chatbot and consult a trained professional.

OPEN-ENDED PROMPTS

Teach me some popular breathing exercises.

How do I calm down when I'm feeling overwhelmed?

Give me a stress-relief routine that will help me sleep.

Build a brain-training puzzle I can print out.

Help me understand how to meditate.

What advice can I give a friend who is depressed?

SPECIFIC PROMPTS

Act as a wellness coach. Guide me through a short, calming exercise I can use right now to manage stress. Keep it practical, easy to follow, and rooted in simple breathing or mindfulness. End with one tip I can use throughout my day.

I have a stressful job interview tomorrow, and I can't stop thinking about it. Come up with five different ways I can turn my brain off and not think about work. Keep them simple, fun, and indoors. Make sure the tone is light and playful.

Give me three reflective journaling prompts that help me process my emotions, track family relationships, and reframe difficulties positively. Make them open-ended and simple to respond to. Add a short reminder of why journaling supports mental health and how I can make it a daily habit.

Act as a gentle check-in buddy. Ask me a few thoughtful questions about how I'm feeling today and suggest healthy coping strategies tailored to my needs. Keep your tone supportive, empathetic, and nonjudgmental. Start by offering a small uplifting reminder for my day.

You are a sleep scientist. Offer me five science-based tips to improve sleep quality, including routines before bed and small lifestyle adjustments during the day. Keep the advice simple and realistic, avoiding overly technical language.

Can you help me find a male therapist in my area who accepts my insurance? Please provide a list of five, including their star review scores on multiple platforms and their specialties. Create it in a bulleted list in a direct and realistic tone.

Give me a set of quick brain exercises I can try right now to strengthen my memory, creativity, and focus. Include a mix of puzzles, word games, and logic challenges. Write a paragraph on how each activity supports cognitive health and suggest how often I should be playing these games.

I want to learn a new skill, but I don't know where to start. Come up with three skills, breaking them into manageable steps and how often I should practice them. Offer encouragement or tips in a positive tone as if you were a Disney character.

You are a wellness coach. Create a realistic daily plan that balances work, rest, and self-care. Use productivity techniques, keep suggestions practical but not overwhelming, and include strategies to prevent burnout.

Suggest thoughtful ways I can strengthen relationships with family or friends this week. Include small acts of kindness, meaningful conversation starters, and fun activities. Keep the tone encouraging and emphasize connection above all. End with one activity I can try today.

Help me create a balanced weekly routine that gives time for work, hobbies, rest, and personal achievements. Suggest ways to structure my time so I'm less burned out. Include reminders to stay flexible and show myself compassion, even if I don't follow the plan perfectly.

Give me three uplifting motivational mantras I can use when I feel stuck or unproductive. Keep the language warm and supportive. They should be spiritual and actionable, including practical knowledge I can use in my everyday life.

I am feeling lonely and would like to have a conversation about my favorite hobby. Act as a big fan of baseball cards and have a conversation with me about your favorite year and set. Keep the tone friendly and joyful without any insults or mean language.

Come up with a series of tools I can use to help manage my anxiety. Include tips, daily activities, and methods to reduce my stress. Come up with a list of sayings I can tell myself when my anxiety gets too strong and include a hotline I can contact if things get dire.

Help me reframe negative thoughts into positive ones. Offer three examples of common unhelpful thoughts and healthier ways to reinterpret them. Use simple, supportive language, and explain how practicing reframing can strengthen resilience over time.

You are a mindfulness coach who focuses on emotional balance. Guide me through a three-minute mindfulness activity I can do at my desk to reset and feel calmer. Use clear, step-by-step instructions, focusing on breath, body awareness, and senses.

Suggest three practical strategies to build my confidence during stressful times. Use simple examples of how I might apply them in everyday life. Keep the advice realistic, encouraging, and free of complicated lingo so I can act on it right away.

Create a bulleted list with five new words or phrases to describe emotions beyond just "good" or "bad." Explain each word briefly and give an example of when I might feel that way. Explain in a paragraph how expanding my emotional vocabulary helps me better understand myself.

Give me five inspiring affirmations I can use to give me a boost at the start of my day. It can be as simple as stepping outside or calling a friend. Keep them light and positive, designed to brighten my life without adding too much unneeded stress.

I am trying to take a break from caffeine, but I'm struggling to do so. Come up with a monthlong plan broken down by day that I can use to keep motivated and energized. Offer alternatives and exercises I can use that won't cost too much time or energy.

HOW CHATGPT CAN HELP WITH RELATIONSHIPS AND DATING

There are many digital barriers today to finding a special someone. From figuring out dating app algorithms to writing flirty and fun text conversations, there's a never-ending slog of worry and troubles. ChatGPT can help cut through the noise and make dating just a little more tolerable.

What you shouldn't do is use the chatbot as a replacement for a human partnership. There have been quite a few AI chatbots designed to combat users' loneliness by showering them with praise and admiration. Such chatbots can be quite dangerous, leading users into a delusional world where they are convinced they are in love with something that cannot feel any emotions.

If you find yourself spending more time with your chatbot than the partner you are trying to woo, then it might be a good idea to put the text prompt down and go on an actual date. But if you just need some tips for adding structure to your dating life, then ChatGPT can be your wingman.

OPEN-ENDED PROMPTS

Help me find a date.

What is the best outfit to wear on a second date?

How should I respond to this text?

Why can't I find the one?

Best place to have a date that isn't dinner and a movie?

Can you help me practice flirting?

SPECIFIC PROMPTS

You are an expert dating coach. I am struggling to approach women and need some opening lines. Come up with five openers I can use, including positive responses for if they want to have a conversation. Don't be harsh or judgmental.

Come up with five different locations near my area that I can use to find a partner, like bars or theaters. Create a bulleted list of locales, including their pros, cons, and best places to hang around. Keep the tone calm and serious.

Give me a list of five locations that would be appropriate for a first date. They should be fairly quiet, not too expensive, and have a low-key vibe. Include conversation topics and responses I can give to questions. End with a pep talk to get me pumped for the date.

I want to buy a gift for my significant other, but I don't know where to start. She loves jewelry and dogs. Come up with a list of items I can purchase under $100, including links and reviews. Keep the tone professional and serious.

My boyfriend and I keep fighting about simple things. Come up with a structured plan I can use to de-escalate fights and come to solutions without anyone getting angry. Keep the tone simple and professional.

I'm trying to figure out what I should wear on a date. Come up with a bulleted list of clothing I can wear, including accessories and shoes. Make sure they aren't too flashy or over the top, but will still impress my date.

You are a relationship coach. My wife refuses to do the dishes, no matter how many times I ask. Come up with a conversation I have that approaches the topic, comes up with a solution, and gets the dishes done once every few days.

I'm going on a date with a vegan and don't know where a good place to go is. Come up with a bulleted list of three options, like museums or restaurants. Include conversations I can have about being a vegan and their childhood.

I realize I have to break up with my partner, but I'm too scared to do so. Help me come up with a structured plan I can follow to end the relationship without hurting their feelings too much. Be straight to the point and mellow, coming up with multiple contingency plans for if things go awry.

You are a sex coach with years of experience. In a nonjudgmental tone, please suggest resources I can use to improve in the bedroom, such as videos or books. Try not to use vulgar language or profanities. I am a very Christian person.

I struggle with texting between dates. Draft a set of text templates I can use to show interest without seeming needy. Keep them light, playful, and tailored to building toward the next date.

It's our fifth anniversary, and I'm looking for a special gift to buy. Give me a list of five gift ideas that signify our half decade together and are special, heartfelt, and personalized. Include their prices, links, and how common a gift they are.

My husband snores quite a lot, and it's becoming a problem. Come up with a detailed plan I can use to approach the topic with him and solutions. Include in a calming tone what causes snoring so I can better understand the problem.

I want to feel more confident when starting conversations on dates. Create a role-play scenario where I practice different openers. Give me feedback on tone and humor, and body language tips to make me sound approachable and genuine.

I'm not very good at dating apps and want to improve. Come up with a list of tips or tricks I can use to improve my dating profile and conversations I have before going on dates. Answer common questions like when we should start texting and how long until we should go on a physical date.

A person I went on a single date with has started to seem distant in their texts. Analyze the conversation up until this point and give me multiple reasons as to why you think they no longer seem interested. Keep the tone serious and answer in detail.

Teach me how to read signals of attraction and comfort during a date. Provide a checklist of body language cues, tone shifts, and small behaviors that indicate whether someone is enjoying themselves or losing interest.

Guide me in setting healthy boundaries in dating. Provide strategies for communicating deal-breakers and preferences respectfully, while staying goal-oriented. Use examples of how I can phrase boundaries without sounding rigid or confrontational.

Help me reframe rejection so it feels acceptable instead of like failure. Create a short pep-talk script I can revisit after an unsuccessful date or unanswered message, with reminders of my self-worth and practical steps forward.

My new girlfriend wants to move in but has several cats. What are some problems that can arise when living with cats if you're not used to them? Come up with solutions to those problems and ways I can learn to be more cat-friendly.

THE TEN BEST PROMPTS IN THIS BOOK

Congratulations on getting to the end of the book and learning how to prompt! With so many ways to use chatbots, I'm sure you'll be improving your life in no time. After writing five hundred new prompts, I've grown attached to quite a few. Here are my top ten favorite prompts and why I'm in love with each.

BEST PROMPT #1

You are an astronaut meeting with aliens for the first time and want to show them the best food on planet Earth. Include food from each part of the globe, making sure they pair well together. Use a sci-fi tone and present each recipe as part of a mission log.

My favorite prompts are always the quirkier ones, which force ChatGPT to come up with something it doesn't normally get asked. Summarizing all of humanity's culinary accomplishments into a list isn't easy, but it managed to come up with some interstellar offerings like Peruvian ceviche and Moroccan lamb tagine with apricots.

BEST PROMPT #2

I'm planning a day trip to New York City with three adventurous friends in August, and I'm looking for an Italian restaurant with outdoor seating that won't be too crowded. Create a bulleted list of five amazing restaurants in Manhattan and Brooklyn that are budget-friendly and offer gluten-free options.

I hate restaurant planning and can easily get overwhelmed with all of the options in a city. Having ChatGPT narrow down the options makes my life a whole lot easier. A prompt like this lets me focus more on eating and less on stressing to make sure that everyone in my party gets exactly what they want. The less wiggle room you give ChatGPT, the better answers it can offer, so prompts with a lot of detail lead to the best results.

BEST PROMPT #3

You are a chef who keeps your pantry beautifully organized at all times. Help me create a pantry inventory system to reduce wasted space. Include food items every chef should have at home, like grains, canned goods, and snacks. Format as a template I can fill in.

When my partner moved into my apartment, she reorganized my pantry in a way I never thought possible. Having all your foods in neat, easily recognizable places allows you to spend less time searching and more time cooking. If you don't have a partner like mine, having ChatGPT create a system that works for you will help eliminate clutter while making your life just a tad bit easier. I like this prompt especially because it can suggest kitchen staples you might not have thought of that you can add to your rotation.

BEST PROMPT #4

I've decided that I'm going to open a cat café and need to teach my employees how to take care of a dozen feisty felines. As a feline behaviorist, write a staff training memo covering body language cues, boundaries, and enrichment best practices. Include how many litter boxes and feeders we'd need and how often they'd have to be checked.

As I'm writing this, there's a cat sprawled across my side asking for cuddles, so I know how demanding taking care of a cat can be. I love this prompt because it gives ChatGPT the parameters to explain a complicated topic while giving it enough information to create a useful answer. Outsourcing your cat café care to a robot wouldn't necessarily be the best for your business, but it would be a good exercise in figuring out how to take care of a couple of feline friends.

BEST PROMPT #5

You are a money-saving specialist. I want to save $300 a month when I make $5,000 and my rent is $2,000. Come up with a bulleted plan to help me put this money aside. Include ways I could cut costs in a mature and mothering tone.

I've never been good at balancing my budget, but ChatGPT has helped me figure out how best to save. Giving it your income and expenses, it can easily output a spreadsheet or chart you can use to figure out the bottom line. This prompt is designed to help you save without making you feel judged. It offers solutions I never would have thought of, like calling up my utility providers and seeing if I can get lower rates.

BEST PROMPT #6

Aliens land in your backyard, but instead of invading, they beg you to help them become TikTok famous. Write the first conversation you have with them, what dances you plan on doing, and how you plan their viral debut.

I love to hand ChatGPT a prompt completely out of left field and see the magic it spits out. This prompt is mostly silly, with aliens describing a step-by-step dance where they whip their arms and legs around like they are trying to get all the views. But in its answer, it also provides practical advice for going viral on TikTok, like using a trending hashtag or audio. It's silly and the closest thing it can do to imagination, bringing TikTok closer to the stars.

BEST PROMPT #7

Design a fabric flag I can create to represent my love for vampires. Come up with a catchy slogan, a single image, and a pattern I can replicate. Break down how much the materials would cost and how long it would take.

Crafting is an inherently creative task, but it can be improved with help from ChatGPT. With this prompt, you'll be able to come up with a series of new projects that would be impossible to devise on the basis of Google or YouTube results without finding a *Twilight* fan page. How else would you think about creating a flag to show your bloodsucker pride?

BEST PROMPT #8

I want to start a hobby, but I don't know which one to pick. Provide me with five different hobbies and list their pros, cons, and associated expenses in a chart. Include mainstream popular options as well as more obscure hobbies I might find interesting.

ChatGPT works best when it's finding solutions to your everyday problems. Hobbies can be incredibly expensive, and you can't really try a bunch of them without investing a ton of capital or finding someone else who already has. The prospect of spending hundreds of dollars on yarn only to learn you hate knitting is a legitimate worry. So, having ChatGPT parse through a bunch of options can mitigate some of that danger, and it can even find something you never would have thought of. After it recommended lockpicking, I opened Amazon and added a locksmith kit to my cart.

BEST PROMPT #9

You are a chess coach teaching me how to be better at the game. Come up with a bulleted list of skills, moves, and techniques that chess grandmasters use that I can replicate. Keep the tone serious as I train for a chess tournament.

Learning new skills is the best way to keep life fresh, but it isn't always easy. Chess has exploded in popularity over the past few years, and many people are learning the classic game. This prompt breaks down the difficult barrier of learning what pieces do, moves, and so much more. If you are serious about chess, you must treat training like it's a physical sport, constantly improving and practicing. Prompts like these help you improve without having to search the internet for new ways to learn.

BEST PROMPT #10

Give me a list of five locations that would be appropriate for a first date. They should be fairly quiet, not too expensive, and have a low-key vibe. Include conversation topics and responses I can give to questions. End with a pep talk to get me pumped for the date.

Though I am no longer in the dating pool, I still remember how terrifying finding a first date location was. You don't want to hit the same spot too many times, or the staff will think you are a player. But you also don't want to pick anything too unfamiliar and get overwhelmed by all the newness in the air. Using ChatGPT like a Google Maps curator allows you to find the answers you need without ending up in a terrifying biker bar or clown-themed restaurant.

Notes

References

"Chatgpt.com September 2025 Traffic Stats." Semrush. semrush.com/website/chatgpt.com/overview/. Accessed September 10, 2025.

"ChatGPT Fundamentals." OpenAI Academy. academy.openai.com/public/clubs/work-users-ynjqu/resources/chatgpt-basics?utm_source=chatgpt.com. Accessed September 10, 2025.

Field, Hayden, and Kate Rooney. "OpenAI Closes $40 Billion Funding Round, Largest Private Tech Deal on Record." CNBC. March 31, 2025. cnbc.com/2025/03/31/openai-closes-40-billion-in-funding-the-largest-private-fundraise-in-history-softbank-chatgpt.html.

"Latest ChatGPT Statistics: 800M+ Users, Revenue (Oct 2025)." NerdyNav. Last updated October 5, 2025. nerdynav.com/chatgpt-statistics/.

Sidoti, Olivia, and Colleen McClain. "34% of U.S. Adults Have Used ChatGPT, About Double the Share in 2023." Pew Research Center. June 25, 2025. pewresearch.org/short-reads/2024/03/26/americans-use-of-chatgpt-is-ticking-up-but-few-trust-its-election-information/.

Sidoti, Olivia, Eugenie Park, and Jeffrey Gottfried. "About a Quarter of U.S. Teens Have Used ChatGPT for Schoolwork—Double the Share in 2023." Pew Research Center. January 15, 2025. pewresearch.org/short-reads/2025/01/15/about-a-quarter-of-us-teens-have-used-chatgpt-for-schoolwork-double-the-share-in-2023/.

Stover, Dawn. "AI Goes Nuclear." *Bulletin of the Atomic Scientists*. December 19, 2024. thebulletin.org/2024/12/ai-goes-nuclear/.

Tan, Kwan Wei Kevin. "Sam Altman Says the Energy Needed for an Average CHATGPT Query Can Power a Lightbulb for a Few Minutes." Business Insider. June 11, 2025. businessinsider.com/how-much-energy-does-chatgpt-use-average-query-watts-altman-2025-6.

Zewe, Adam. "Explained: Generative AI's Environmental Impact." MIT News. January 17, 2025. news.mit.edu/2025/explained-generative-ai-environmental-impact-0117.

Index

Acknowledgments

Thank you to my lovely partner, to my editor, and to the world that has created such wonderful technology.

About the Author

Stanley Lieber has been a journalist covering the internet and technology for many different outlets over the past decade. Living in New York with multiple cats, he's spent years watching technology grow while studying it up close. He cares a lot about the internet and the culture that exists within it, spending multiple hours a day on social media, scouring the pages for the next big scoop.